Youth Spirit

PROGRAM IDEAS FOR CHURCH GROUPS

Collected from over 10 years of the
phenomenal Christian education
curriculum and worship resource
The Whole People of God, these
volumes offer tried and true material in easy-to-use format. These are
proven resources with a theology
and approach that thousands have
come to trust.

PROGRAM IDEAS FOR CHURCH GROUPS

Youth Spirit

WOOD
LAKE
BOOKS

Editor: Anne Saunders
Cover design: Lois Huey-Heck, Margaret Kyle
Consulting art director: Robert MacDonald
Cover photograph: Kent Lindsey Photography, hand-colored by Lois Huey-Heck

At **Wood Lake Books**, we practice what we publish, guided by a concern for fairness, justice, and equal opportunity in all of our relationships with employees and customers.

Canadian Cataloguing in Publication Data

Perry, Cheryl, 1970 –
   Youth spirit

   Includes bibliographical references and
index.
   ISBN 1-55145-247-2

   1. Church group work with you 2.
Christian education — Activity programs.
I. Saunders, Anne, 1951 – II. Title.
BC4447.P47 1996   259'.23C96-910389-1

Printing 10 9 8 7 6 5 4 3

Published by Wood Lake Books
10162 Newene Road
Winfield, BC V4V 1R2

Printed in Canada by
Blitz Print

Contents

Acknowledgments

I wish to acknowledge and thank the following people for their contributions to this book: Nancy Nourse, for her ideas for "Love" and "Violence and the Media," AnnaLisa Bond for her ideas for "Identity and Self-Esteem," Tressa Brotsky for "The Genesis Story," and the development team of *The Whole People of God* curriculum. Special thanks to Marilyn Perry, for her guidance and support, and to Anne Saunders for editing the manuscript. I wish to express my gratitude to Dave, my partner, and to Toni, Chris, Scott, Jane and Michelle – my fellow youth group leaders – who gave me their moral support while I worked on this book. Lastly, I wish to express my thanks to the many young people who have been in youth groups I've led over the years. You have been as much my companions as I have been yours on this journey we call faith. Shalom!

Cheryl Perry

How to Use This Book

This book provides creative program ideas for youth groups and their leaders. Some of the material has been adapted from "Youth Paks" of *The Whole People of God* curriculum. Some of it has come from the shared experiences of people working weekly with "real life" youth groups.

We have organized the material according to themes on "Idea Pages." These pages encourage leaders to "pick and choose" activities, building their own unique programs. We suggest a method for doing this in the Introduction. Each Idea Page offers a variety of suggestions. These include games, crafts, discussion starters, reflection questions, and project ideas, as well as a group check-in and a closing worship.

These Idea Pages are grouped into sections according to the seasons of the Christian Year. Each section begins with a description of the season – its mood and flavor, special days, and implications for youth. Many denominations organize their worship and church life following the Christian Year and the lectionary. With this book organized

in the same way, we hope you will easily find activities to involve your group in the life and work of the larger church community. The book begins with the Season after Pentecost. This coincides with early autumn in North America when school reconvenes after summer holidays and most youth programs are starting up.

Stories, graphics, descriptions of games and projects, and worship materials appear throughout the book with some additional resources in the final section. These resources complement the Idea Pages. All of them can be reproduced for use with the youth in your church. Permission must be requested to photocopy materials for other purposes. We have also included an annotated bibliography on youth ministry and cross-referenced indexes.

We hope this book will help you create meaningful and spirited programs for your youth group. May the Spirit guide you in this challenging, fun, and important ministry!

Introduction to Planning and Implementing Youth Programs

Learning Together

Learning is a lifelong process. From birth to death we are changing and growing. Whether we're children, youth, or adults, we all have experiences that help us grow in our understanding of ourselves, our relationships with others, and our relationship with God.

At all ages we can learn from one another; at all ages we can teach one another. As youth leaders we don't need to be the "experts." We can learn from, and along with, the young people in the group. Young people appreciate leaders who are:

- Honest about their own stage of spiritual growth
- Open to learning from, and with, young people
- Willing to risk expressing their own concerns, questions, and beliefs
- Willing to really listen
- Committed to giving their time to prepare for, and attend, youth group meetings.

Youth consider these qualities far more important than having the "right" answers. We hope many of the activities in this book will help youth group members form relationships of trust, openness, and acceptance – with each other and with their leaders. Such relationships will enable them to explore their beliefs and feelings together.

The Developmental Needs of Youth

Many books give detailed information about the developmental stages of youth and the implications of these for youth ministry (see Annotated Bibliography). In their research for "Young Adolescents and Their Communities: a Shared Responsibility," William Kerewsky and Leah M. Lefstein* suggest that young people have the following seven developmental needs:

- Competence and achievement
- Creative expression
- Meaningful participation
- Physical activity
- Positive social interaction with peers and adults
- Self-definition
- Structure and clear limits

Kerewsky and Lefstein acknowledge the enormous developmental diversity among young adolescents. They conclude that youth require a variety of types and levels of activities designed to meet these seven needs. Few youth programs can meet all seven needs at once. Recognizing this, Kerewsky and Lefstein suggest planning programs that meet a minimum of four developmental needs in each program, and trying to vary these four from program to program.

* From *3:00 to 6:00 P.M.: Young Adolescents at Home in the Community*, Carrboro: University of North Carolina, 1982.

Youth and the Learning Process

Learning usually follows a sequential process. You have an experience, you reflect on it, and you try to integrate the newly gained knowledge into your life. As Christians, we know we are never alone in this process. God is part of all our learning.

The **Idea Pages** in this book include ideas for creating programs based on this learning process (an "action-reflection-integration" model).

Each **Idea Page** includes suggestions for the following five program elements:

1. Check-in

The starting point in the learning process consists of a person's life experiences, knowledge, talents, values, and needs. We are more likely to provide programs that meet the needs and interests of our group members if we have some understanding of their physical, spiritual, emotional, and social development. Some of this may come from reading books. Most of it will come from personal relationships with the youth in your group. Take time to learn about the goals, abilities, interests, and concerns of your group members. (See Feature YOU-th Project in Section F.)

2. Experiences

Both the planned and the unexpected, the "good break" and the "stroke of bad luck," provide significant experiences in our lives. They spark change and growth in us. Young people can have significant experiences during retreats, Bible study, service projects, a closing meditation, and in their everyday lives – with an unusual dream, the death of a friend, an award for personal achievement. As leaders, we can create opportunities for youth to have experiences that will encourage spiritual growth. We can also design youth programs that respond to the day-to-day experiences of concern to our members. Be open and flexible, ready to adapt activities to suit your group.

3. Reflection

Reflection involves analyzing and reflecting on our experiences. It may involve gathering more information or having another experience. Reflection can include solitary activities like praying, guided meditation, and journal writing, as well as interactive situations like small group discussions, role plays, and research. People gain insights by reflecting on experiences. These may come as a sudden "aha!" during the experience or they may develop slowly.

4. Integration

Integration involves applying new learning by doing. Through self-expression, youth make the connection between their new insights and their day-to-day realities. In planning youth programs, we can select activities like projects, games, and crafts to help youth apply their faith discoveries to their everyday lives.

5. Closing Worship

In worship youth have opportunities to recognize and feel God's presence in their lives. Worship can include scripture, prayer, music, and rituals. You may want to have worship at the beginning, the end, or at both times in your program.

Designing Youth Programs

With the learning process as our guideline and the **Idea Pages** as a resource, we can design programs that meet the developmental needs of our group members. We suggest following the following steps:

IdeaPage

1. Choose an Idea Page theme for the program and decide your program goals.
2. Decide how to do the "Group Check-In." Use the one suggested on the Idea Page, adapt it, or substitute another.
3. Choose activities from the Idea Page for each of these learning stages:
   Experience
   Reflection
   Integration
4. Add a couple of the group's favorite games or other activities that relate to the theme.
5. Include a worship. Each Idea Sheet has suggestions for "Closing Worship"* that can be adapted to begin or end your program.
6. Review your whole program outline to confirm that the activities meet at least four developmental needs. If you are not satisfied, consider ways to adapt activities.

Using this method, we prepared the sample program outline on the next page. (A blank outline follows for you to copy and use for designing your own programs.) We chose "Idea Page #2 – Group Building with Hands and Feet" from Section A: The Season after Pentecost.

When you review your program outline, check off the needs that the program will meet. After every youth group meeting or event, take a moment to evaluate what happened, noting comments on the form. After several weeks, look back over these forms and ask these questions:

- Do the programs I design meet the same developmental needs each time?
- If so, which needs am I ignoring? How can I meet these needs?
- Do I need to adapt activities more often to meet specific needs of members in this group?

Use your evaluation comments and your answers to these questions to help you improve the design of future programs.

*Add your own musical options to the worship (and to other parts of the program), drawing on the traditions of your denomination. Encourage musically talented group members to assist, and make use of the music and equipment available in your church.

PROGRAM OUTLINE
(Example Only)

GROUP NAME: Unique Minds (Grades 7 and Up)
DATE: Nov. 1997

THEME: Group Building

Goals: – to explore "where we've been" as a group so far this year
– to explore what it means to be a "Christian Community"
– to do some long-range planning

Group Check-in: – use suggested "choosing part of the body"
– need to do some additional checking-in because we didn't meet last week

Experience:
Footprint Banner

Needed:
• paint, aluminum pie plates, sponges, banner paper, buckets, towels
• newspaper, masking tape

Reflection:
– focusing more on where we've been and where we're headed
– group members will add symbols of whate we've done and what they hope to do.

Needed:

Integration:
Foot-long sundae

Needed:
• phone group to ask them to bring favorite toppings, buy ice cream
• lightweight cardboard, tin foil, wax paper

Other:
Twister
People to People (group version)

Needed:
• Game (Michelle?)

Closing Worship:
• Use water-soluble crayons to make fish shapes on the backs of hands
"we're glad you're part of our group and ..."

Needed:
• water-soluble crayons

This program addresses these developmental needs:
- ○ physical activity
- ○ competence and achievement
- ○ self-definition
- ○ creative expression
- ○ positive social interaction
- ○ structure and clear limits
- ○ meaningful participation

Evaluation
Did the program meet your goals? _____
_____

What worked well and what didn't? _____
_____
_____

PROGRAM OUTLINE

GROUP NAME:

DATE:

THEME:

Goals:

Group Check-in:

Experience:	**Needed:**
Reflection:	**Needed:**
Integration:	**Needed:**
Other:	**Needed:**
Closing Worship:	**Needed:**

This program addresses these developmental needs:
- ○ physical activity
- ○ competence and achievement
- ○ self-definition
- ○ creative expression
- ○ positive social interaction
- ○ structure and clear limits
- ○ meaningful participation

Evaluation

Did the program meet your goals? _____
_____

What worked well and what didn't? _____
_____
_____

Getting Off the Ground

Whether starting up a new group or bringing youth back together, take time to think about how you will contact individuals. Are there one or two key youth who are willing and available to work with you to get the group going? Ask for their ideas and their help. Together collect the names and addresses of all potential group members. Ask for names from your clergy, church school workers, church directory, and from young people themselves. Send out invitations to everyone on your list. Then follow up with a phone call personally inviting them to the first group meeting. Encourage everyone to bring along friends.

For your first meeting, plan a non-threatening, social gathering – one where youth will feel comfortable bringing along their friends. They will also find it easier to get to know one another. Plan the event for early autumn when young people are deciding which extracurricular activities, sports teams, and groups they want to join.

Advertise! Advertise! Advertise!

Be creative in your advertising. Use lots of graphics including those found in this book. Ask permission to put up posters at local schools and places where youth gather in your community. Advertise on a television station that gives free space to community groups.

If your church puts out a newsletter or personal letter from the clergy before the end of the summer, or has a home page on the "Net," include information about the youth group and its programs. Set up an information table in the narthex or church hall after worship. Display information and pictures of the youth group from previous years.

The key is lots of visibility and lots of advertising – at the start-up and throughout the year.

Building Relationships with Youth Group Members

Often we make a difference in the lives of young people through the personal relationships we build with them. Our concern, our willingness to listen, and the interest we take in their lives can have an affirming and lasting impression. How do youth leaders build and maintain relationships with group members throughout the year? Keeping in touch with youth takes an investment of time and energy, but it is a key component in youth ministry. Here are suggestions to help you:

- **Phone regularly.** The telephone is perhaps the most effective way of communicating with youth (though e-mail is gaining in popularity). Sometimes you may need to make phone calls to remind youth of group plans or to bring something. These provide opportunities to connect with members. Call on birthdays, when someone has been absent, or just to say "hi." Remember – you don't always need a reason for calling.

- **Keep notes.** Write the name, address, birth date, and telephone number of each group member on a recipe card along with any known interests or hobbies. Keep these updated. When you have a telephone conversation, have the person's card in front of you. For example, if a youth tells you they are preparing for a difficult exam, write this down. The next time you call, followup with them by asking about the exam. Be sure you keep all information confidential.

  Name: _____
  Phone #: _____
  Likes: _____

- **Organize a project.** Try an ongoing project like **Feature YOU-th** described in the Section F: Resources. This will help you get to know youth members better.

- **Send postcards.** When you're away on holidays, send postcards to the youth in your group. Over the summer, encourage the youth to keep in touch with you by sending postcards from places they visit. Make a display of these at the end of the summer.

- **Publish a newsletter.** Send out a regular newsletter that lets youth know about upcoming events and describes things you've done as a group. Include lots of graphics and cartoons. Invite youth to contribute their own art. Encourage them to let their families read the newsletter, too.

- **Prepare monthly calendars.** Photocopy the **Calendar** in Section F: Resources for group members. Have everyone record the meeting times and dates, group members' birthdays and upcoming special events. Encourage the youth to put these on the refrigerator door so their parents will also have this information.

Mark It on Your Calendar!

- **Maintain a youth bulletin board.** Arrange to use a bulletin board centrally located in your church for youth news. Put up a wipe-off, wall calendar that shows an overview of two months or the whole year for parents and youth to consult.

- **Recognize birthdays.** Phone youth on their birthdays or plan as a group to recognize them. At the beginning of the year ask each member if they want to buy a small gift under five dollars, wrap it, and put it in a "birthday box." When someone has a birthday they choose a gift from the box. Or youth might agree to bake birthday cakes. When the first member of the group has a birthday someone agrees to bake a cake. The person who had the birthday cake baked for them provides the cake for the next birthday, and so on. Be sure to recognize in some way the birthdays that happen over the summer.

- **Organize special outings.** A meeting away from the church – at a bowling alley, swimming pool, or skating rink – provides an opportunity for you to relax and enjoy getting to know group members in a different setting. Invite the youth to your home for a special program like a video show with popcorn.

Videos and Youth Groups

Videos can be wonderful learning tools and great discussion starters for youth. Careful preparation and planning ensure their effectiveness. Build in program time not only for viewing the video, but also for debriefing and discussing issues raised by it. This is particularly critical if the movie explores difficult or disturbing subject matter. Extend the normal program time to allow for this. Feature-length films are usually too long to view and discuss in a regular-length program. Incorporate viewing and discussing a film into a sleepover or evening at a youth group member's home; or choose to show only a clip of the video to start discussion (especially if this is a movie many of the youth have already seen).

Commercially sold films and videos from rental outlets* are licensed "for home use only." A church, or anywhere other than a private home, is considered a "public place." Showing them in such places violates the law. Some church youth groups have been fined.

You can show these videos outside of the home only with permission from the copyright holder or film distributor. You may gain permission from the distributor by phoning them directly, or by purchasing a license from a company such as Audio Cine Films (1-800-289-8887 or www.acf-film.com); or the Motion Picture Licensing Corporation, which represents 40 production companies – Disney and Warner Bros. and many religious video distributors (1-800-462-8855 or www.mplc.com). If your church has an adult video discussion group, several youth groups, and church school classes that like to use videos, you may want to explore this option.

---

*Videos rented or purchased from church outlets, which are licensed for educational use, do not carry these restrictions.

Tips for Using a Video As An Educational Tool With Youth

- Screen the video carefully beforehand. Do not rely on others' recommendations or a vague recollection of having seen the film yourself and thinking it was suitable.

- Consider the ages and developmental stages of the youth audience. Is the subject matter appropriate? Will it interest them? What is your purpose in showing the video? Imagine some of your group members going home and giving a synopsis of the film to a parent. How might parents react? If you have a support group made up of parents who have youth in the group, make sure they understand why you are choosing to view this film and what you hope to accomplish with it. They can help reassure other parents and adults in the congregation who might be skeptical.

- If you want the group to view only part of the film, preview it and note segments you might use as a "clip" to start discussion. Showing one or two clips may be a good compromise when a thought-provoking film contains scenes unsuitable for youth viewers.

- Create a list of questions to guide discussion. Write these on newsprint and display them before beginning the video. Encourage youth to refer to them from time to time. Alternatively, photocopy the list for each member, asking them to record their own responses and discuss them with a partner when the movie ends. A list of questions can guide youth while viewing the movie and increase their awareness as an audience. If you are renting videos from a church outlet, ask for a list of discussion questions and a copy of the study guide whenever these are available.

- Introduce the video to the youth. Give them an idea of the film's subject matter. If the movie contains scenes that might make some youth uncomfortable, warn them about these. (Movies that touch on "disturbing" or difficult subjects do not necessarily need to be excluded. Youth can be given information to help them choose whether or not to watch them.)

Graphics For Youth Newsletters & Other Communications

Mark It on Your Calendar!

Mark It on Your Calendar!

Coming Soon!

Coming Soon!

Section A: Season after Pentecost

Mood and Flavor of the Season

The Season after Pentecost is the longest season in the Christian Year. It stretches from Pentecost Sunday in late May or early June to Reign of Christ Sunday at the end of November. During this time we celebrate the growth of the Church after Pentecost. We also explore how we can be the hands and feet of Christ, carrying on his work in the world. The liturgical color of the season is green, symbolizing growth.

Scripture readings during this season have a strong social justice flavor, calling us to live with concern for our neighbor. In the Season after Pentecost we take time to dream of a world of wholeness, harmony, and peace; we imagine God's reign of Shalom happening in today's world. We reflect on how we live in community, how we accept and support one another, and how we grow together in God's way.

Special Days

In autumn we think about Thanksgiving Sunday, but there are other special days. Christians around the world celebrate Worldwide Communion Sunday on the first Sunday of October. World Food Day is October 16. October 24 marks the anniversary of the United Nations and the start of Disarmament Week. Peace Sabbath also falls in October. Remembrance or Veterans' Day is November 11 and the month of November is Holocaust Month. Prisoners' Sunday also falls in November. These are not part of the Christian Year, but many churches recognize them as expressions of our vision and commitment as Christians.

The liturgical festival of All Saints also occurs during this season. We remember people throughout history who have worked for the transformation of the Church, society, and our world. Halloween, or All Hallows' Eve, is a part of the three-day celebration that includes All Hallows' Eve, All Saints' Day, and All Souls' Day.

The Season after Pentecost ends with Reign of Christ Sunday. On this last Sunday in the Christian Year we commit ourselves again to work for God's reign in our world.

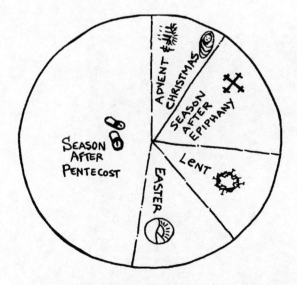

The Season after Pentecost is the longest season in the Christian Year.

Implications for Youth Ministry

The mood and flavor of the Season after Pentecost suggest many rich themes and program possibilities.

The theme of community is an important one for youth groups, especially at this time of year when most groups are beginning. This season provides opportunities to build community within your own group as well as within the larger community. Doing projects together, perhaps focusing on the issues of world hunger, disarmament, and peace, can help build a sense of community in your group. At the same time these projects can benefit the larger community.

As groups are forming, youth need to get to know one another and develop a sense of group identity. Group members may play name games and trust exercises, create some group "standards" of behavior, and plan future programs together.

The Idea Pages in this section include suggestions to help you build a sense of belonging and acceptance in your group. Take time to build relationships of trust between group members – these will create the foundation on which you build programs for the rest of the year.

Forming Community

Group Check-in

Play the game **Feelings** (like the card game Pit™). Prepare the **Feelings Cards** on page 21 and give everyone two cards. The object is to obtain cards that describe how you're feeling. On the leader's signal, everyone moves into the center of the circle and begins trading one or both of their cards (held face down) by shouting "one!" or "two!" (depending on the number of cards they wish to trade). They must find someone who wants to trade the same number of cards. Once a successful trade has been made, players look at the new cards they have. If these don't reflect how they're feeling, they continue trading. If only one of the cards describes how they're feeling, they hold on to that one and trade the other card with someone who also wants to trade "one!" When a player has two cards that describe how they're feeling, they sit down. When everyone has finished trading, sit in a circle and take turns saying which cards you have and why you're feeling that way.

Name Bingo or Signature Squares

When new groups are first forming, both youth and leaders may feel uncomfortable and unsure. These games help "break the ice" and help people get better acquainted. See instructions on page 22.

Name Acrostics

Hand out pieces of paper and markers. Invite everyone to write their names in large block letters in the center of the page. Have them pair up. Suggest a topic for discussion (e.g. school activities, life at home, food). Give partners two minutes to talk to one another (each one talks for a minute).

Then instruct them to exchange papers. Using a letter of their partner's name to create the word, ask everyone to write down one thing they learned or observed about their partner from their discussion. Repeat the process with different partners and different discussion topics until all the letters in their name have been used. (For those with short names, partners may use letters in the words others have written.) In this way group members learn each other's names and something about the others in the group.

Hopes and Hope-Nots

Each member of the group is a unique individual with different talents and interests. How will the group work to include everyone? What ideas do group members have for activities and projects? What would they like to see the group do this year? What do they hope will happen this year? What do they hope will **not** happen?

Brainstorm ideas and record them on newsprint; or provide markers and invite them to record their own ideas on large sheets titled "Hopes" and "Hope-Nots."

Human Knots, Shoe Swap, or Sardines

These are cooperative games that can help members build relationships with each other. See instructions on page 22.

Youth Time and Talents

Hand out copies of the **Youth Time and Talents Form** (on page 23). Give everyone a few minutes to complete these. The information these provide about group members' interests and hobbies can help a leader design successful programs. This also helps everyone get involved in the planning process.

Pair – Pear

This game provides a quick way for group members to pair up and get to know each other. Write some word pairs on paper and cut these apart. Make one half slip per person and put them in a container. Ask everyone to draw a slip. On the leader's signal, members begin searching for the person with the matching half.

Here are some examples of pairs:
- Famous pairs. Simon and Garfunkel, C-3P0 and R2-D2, Lois Lane and Superman
- Biblical figures. David and Goliath, Mary and Joseph, Cain and Abel
- Opposites. Hot and cold, salt and pepper
- Homonyms. Pair and pear, hair and hare
- Periodic Table. H_2O and water, CO_2 and carbon dioxide
- Sounds. Tick and tock, ping and pong
- Fairy tales. Aladdin and the Lamp, Goldilocks and the Three Bears

What do you do once everyone has found their match? Use your imagination! Have partners tell each other something about themselves like where they were born or their favorite movie.

Creating Your Space

If the group has a special space (a meeting room, a bulletin board or wall space), brainstorm about how to decorate it. See **A "Youth Only" Space** on page 24 for ideas. Take some time to plan and assign tasks.

Do You Know Your Neighbor?

This active game helps group members learn each other's names and burn off a little energy!

Instructions:

Sit in a circle. Ask a volunteer (Player #1) to stand in the center. Player #1 chooses someone in the circle (Player #2) and says, "(name of Player #2), do you know your neighbors?" Player #2 responds, pointing to the person on their right and left (Players A and B), saying their names: "Do you mean (name of Player A) and (name of Player B)?" Player #1 responds: "Yes, I mean (name of Player A) and (name of Player B). Do you like your neighbors?" Player #2 can respond either "Yes" or "No, I like the neighbors of (name of another player sitting in the circle)."

- If Player #2 responds with a "Yes" everyone else in the circle except for themselves and Players A and B must get up and find a new seat. Player #1 will try to claim a seat, too. The person left without a seat stands in the center of the circle and play continues.
- If Player #2 responds "No, I like the neighbors of (name of another player sitting in the circle)" the people sitting to the right and left of that player must exchange seats with Players A and B. Player #1 also tries to claim a seat and the person left without a seat stands in the center of the circle and play continues.

Closing Worship

Related Scripture Passage: Acts 2:44–47a.

Squeeze Prayer: (*Read about "Squeeze Prayers" in* Praying with Youth *on page 122.)* The Book of Acts describes how early Christians lived and worshiped together. We have spent some time today getting to know each other. We are beginning to feel like a group or community. During the closing prayer add your own silent or spoken prayers for this group.

O God, as we gather together as a community we are aware of your presence.
We ask you to help us create a caring atmosphere where everyone feels welcome.
(*Each person in turn adds their prayer and then squeezes the hand of the next person.
When the squeeze returns to the first person, they say "Amen" and everyone responds
"Amen."*)

Feelings Cards

Instructions: Photocopy this page, mount on cardboard backing if you wish, and cut apart the squares. Make enough cards so that each group member has at least two cards. See the instructions for playing the **Feelings** game on page 19.

✂ *cut apart on lines*

serious	angry	down	disappointed
thoughtful	included	content	shy
excited	tired	open	silly
awesome	sad	so-so	stunned
friendly	ordinary	confused	OK
happy	fantastic	unsure	worried
stressed out	bummed out	left out	funny
lazy	excellent	foggy	willing
playful	curious	nervous	frustrated
attentive	troubled	grateful	quiet

Games! Games! Games!

Name Bingo

This game works best with groups of five or more. It's a great way to help group members learn each other's name.

Instructions: Copy the **Game Cards** in Section F. Give a card to each group member. Ask everyone to introduce themselves, using their first name only. Ask group members to write everyone's name down on one square of their bingo card. Repeat names if the group is small. They may include their own names. Write names randomly so that everyone's card is different. Write the names of group members on separate slips of paper and place these in a container. Mix them up and draw one, reading the name aloud. Group members may mark an "X" through that square on their bingo card. (If the name appears twice on their card they put an "X" through only one square.) Continue drawing names until someone has "Bingo" (i.e. a completed line running across, diagonally, or horizontally on their bingo card). Award prizes.

Signature Squares

This game is a great mixer and a fun way for group members to learn more about each other.

Instructions: Copy the **Game Card** in Section F. In the squares, write some descriptive phrases (see the samples listed below or make up your own) leaving room in each square for a signature. Then copy the filled-in card. Hand out a card and pen to everyone. Ask them to go around to each other to find people who fit the descriptions and to get their signatures. (Group members shouldn't sign their own cards.)

Encourage everyone to get as many different signatures as possible and to fill in every box. Stop the activity when someone has filled in their entire card. Read out the descriptions and find out who fits each one. (Several people may fit each description.)

Sample Descriptions

- Someone who has blue eyes.
- Someone who can hum the "Mission Impossible" theme.
- Someone who is a vegetarian.
- Someone who has seen "Jesus Christ Superstar."
- Someone who is a member of a sports team.
- Someone who has more than three siblings.
- Someone who has been part of another youth group.
- Someone who has their driver's license.

Human Knots

This game is for five or more people.

Instructions: Stand in a circle. Ask everyone to reach across the circle and join hands with two different people. (Note: Don't join hands with the people on either side of you or take both hands of one person.) Undo the knot by stepping over arms and ducking under arms.

Don't drop hands, but do let hands rotate in a twisting situation. Have group members give suggestions of how people can move in order to untangle the knot. You're finished when everyone is standing in a circle again.

Shoe Swap

This game is for 4 to 8 people.

Instructions: Group members take off both shoes and put them in a pile. Ask everyone to select two different shoes, a right one and a left one. Invite group members to put the mismatched shoes on carefully. (If the shoes are smaller than your feet you will need to balance your toes inside so that you don't ruin someone else's shoes.)

Now find the matching shoes! One person begins with the two people who have shoes that match. Stand between them and place the matching shoe inside the leg of each person in the correct left or right position. Then the next two people join in, positioning their matching shoes. You will need to work together and support each other to be able to match up the pairs. Then celebrate your cooperative achievement!

Sardines

This game works best with larger groups.

Instructions: The object of the game is for the whole group to find the hiding spot of "It." Ask a volunteer to be "It" and to hide. Ask "It" to find a hiding spot that others can squeeze into with them. Be sure to indicate what parts of your meeting space are "off limits." Give "It" enough time to hide before the others go out to find them.

When someone finds "It," they join in hiding and waiting quietly for others to find them. As more and more people find "It," people get a little crowded – like sardines in a can!

Youth Time and Talents Form

Name: _____

Some of my talents include (check any that apply):

☐ singing

☐ taking care of younger
children/baby-sitting

☐ playing a musical instrument

☐ speaking/studying another language

☐ playing sports

☐ writing (articles, poems, prayers
or short stories)

☐ have my driver's license

☐ member of a church/school
committee/club

☐ sewing

☐ leading programs for
children/young people

☐ know First Aid

☐ am a good listener

☐ painting/drawing

☐ acting

☐ public speaking

☐ using a computer

☐ operating audio-visual or sound
equipment

☐ baking/cooking

☐ visiting with elderly people/shut-ins

☐ phoning/talking on the telephone

☐ know lots of games

☐ taking pictures

☐ touching the tip of my nose with
my tongue (hey, this takes real
talent!)

My other interests, hobbies and talents include:

_____

_____

_____

_____

_____

A "Youth Only" Space

Try one of these ideas for making your meeting room look like it's a "youth only" space.

- **Decorate your space.** Ask youth to bring something from home – something that symbolizes who they are – to use in decorating your meeting space. Or you might draft a letter asking for permission to paint a mural of symbols on one of the walls.

- **Create a wall for thoughtful writing.** Cover a wall of your meeting space with newsprint. Encourage youth to write thoughts and feelings on these whenever they wish. (See suggestions below for a "Wailing Wall.")

- **Create a bulletin board** for "youth news." Include a calendar of events and meeting times. Invite youth to add newspaper clippings, photos, art, cartoons, or things they've written.

A "Wailing" Wall

Make one wall of the youth room into a wall like the Western Wall in Jerusalem. Jewish people write their "wailings" – their prayers or concerns – on pieces of paper. Then they leave them in chinks between the stones of this special wall.

Hang or tape up a sheet of heavy plastic. Provide erasable markers (used for writing on overhead transparencies). Mark off stones or bricks on the "wall."

Encourage youth to write or illustrate their "wailings." These can be prayers, things happening in the world, names of people they are concerned about, and anything else that they think belongs there.

Set aside time for this in every program. Design a special closing at the end of the year that includes washing away the accumulated "wailings," offering thanks for God's presence and guidance, praising God for prayers answered and celebrating the caring community of the group.

Group Building with Hands and Feet

Group Check-in

Ask everyone to choose a part of the body that describes how they are feeling. Invite them to explain their choice (e.g. "Right now I'm feeling a bit like a nose...just taking everything in").

Footprint Name Tags

As everyone arrives, give out foot-shaped name tags. Some people may want to personalize these by stamping toes on (by inking their index finger and thumb). Cut these from several different colors of construction paper. Then use the color code to encourage members of the group to mix (e.g. all those with green name tags will clean up after an activity).

Footprint Banner

Group members can go barefoot and create this banner together. Then hang it in your meeting space. See **Footprint Banner** on page 28 for instructions.

Traveling by Foot

Our footprints, like our fingerprints, are totally unique – God hasn't made two exactly alike! Talk about how every person is unique and important to the group. How can such a group of unique people "walk" together? Reflect on traveling in different and new directions as a group this year. What things would they like to see happen for the group? What kinds of things would they like to do? What dreams do they have for the group?

Group Standards

Ask for everyone's suggestions to establish some group "norms" or standards for behavior. Incorporate these into a statement and post this somewhere where it will be visible throughout the year.

Twister

Play the game of Twister™ if someone in the group can bring it from home.

Wanted Poster

Take Polaroid pictures of group members' hands and feet. Design a "Wanted" poster. Include information about where these hands and feet are frequently seen (e.g. in the church hall), what they are seen doing (e.g. name a youth group activity), when last seen (e.g. at youth group on...), and an anonymous tips line. Include the caption "Have you seen these feet?" Make a border using group members' thumbprints.

People to People

Instructions: For this game group members pair up. The leader calls out two body parts (e.g. elbow to knee or toe to toe). Partners then try to connect these body parts (e.g. my elbow to your knee). When the leader calls out "People to People," everyone finds a new partner.

Try a variation of the same game. Have members of the group line up. Call out two body parts that the first two people (A and B) need to connect. Then call out two more. The second person (B) and a third person (C) then try to connect those parts (while B stays connected to A), and so on until the whole group is connected.

The Church – the Body of Christ

In Corinthians 12:12-27, the Apostle Paul used the "body" as a metaphor for the early Church. If we used the same metaphor today, what part of the body do you think youth would represent? Why? Paul wrote to a community that was divided with members arguing a lot. What does this metaphor say about "being community"? How do you think this might apply to our group? What might we need to do in order to make everyone feel a part of the group?

Foot-Long Sundae

Contact group members ahead of time and ask them to bring their favorite ice cream sundae topping (enough for several people).
Instructions: Make a "trough" several feet long using cardboard and tinfoil. Set out on a long table. Place scoops of vanilla ice cream in the trough. Check the ingredients that group members have brought. If members of the group are allergic to any, do not include these. Add ingredients, give everyone a spoon, and dig in!

This is a group effort that can foster discussion about the importance of recognizing and taking into consideration special needs (e.g. allergies) of group members.

Strategy

Play this cooperative game using group members' hands and feet.
Instructions: The object of the game is for group members to get one less foot on the floor, and one more hand on the floor, than there are people in the group. For example, with five people you want to have four feet and six hands on the floor.

Work together to support one another. Try this game with various combinations of hands and feet.

Goin' My Way?

Instructions: Begin this game by forming a circle with two volunteers in the center. Hand them a slip of paper describing an action and have them read it silently. Explain to the rest of the group that this action involves a form of traveling which they are to identify.

The volunteers in the center of the circle begin pantomiming the action. They can add appropriate sound effects, but they can't talk. After a minute invite into the circle a youth who knows the action being pantomimed. They can "travel along" with the other two by pantomiming the actions. When everyone has figured it out and joined in the fun, ask for two new volunteers and start the trip again.

Here are some suggested modes of travel:
• an elevator
• a roller coaster
• an escalator
• a rocket that's taking off
• a time machine
• a leaky canoe
• a city bus
• a skateboard

Closing Worship

Scripture passage: 1 Corinthians 12:12-27
Guided Meditation: Use Margaret Fishback Power's poem **Footprints** on the next page.
Ritual: Use oil to anoint one another with the mark of the cross (on the forehead or back of hand). Have group members anoint one another saying, "(the person's name), we're glad you are a part of our group and a part of Christ's body, the Church."

Footprints

One night I dreamed a dream.
I was walking along the beach with my Lord.
Across the dark sky flashed scenes from my life.
For each scene, I noticed two sets
of footprints in the sand,
one belonging to me
and one to my Lord.
When the last scene of my life shot before me
I looked back at the footprints in the sand.
There was only one set of footprints.
I realized that this was at the lowest
and saddest times of my life.
This always bothered me
and I questioned the Lord
about my dilemma.
"Lord, you told me when I decided to follow You,
You would walk and talk with me all the way.
But I'm aware that during the most troublesome
times of my life there is only one set of footprints.
I just don't understand why, when I needed You most,
You leave me."
He whispered, "My precious child,
I love you and will never leave you
never, ever, during your trials and testings.
When you saw only one set of footprints
it was then that I carried you."

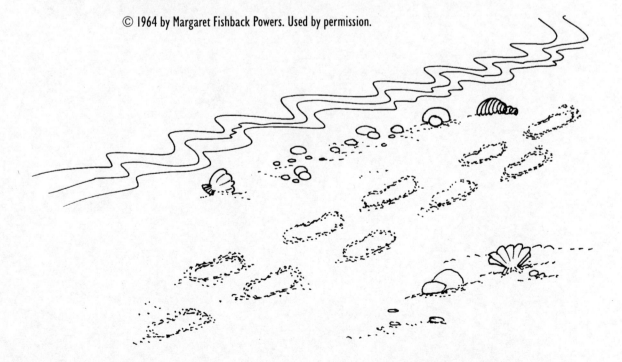

Footprint Banner

You will need: newspaper, masking tape, strips of banner paper, aluminum pie plates, several colors of tempera paint, bucket of soapy water and towels.

Instructions: Cover the oor space with lots of newspaper and tape down. Lay a long strip of banner paper over the top and tape down. Lay extra sheets of newspaper down at each end of the banner. Pour about 1 in. (2.5cm) of paint in pie plates. You may need a re-inking station half-way if your banner is long.

Remove shoes and socks. Ink feet well. Try making prints going different directions; add a sneaker print; or make a baby footprint using a fist and inking the side of the hand and adding toe prints with the thumb and index finger.

Idea Page #3

Trust

Group Check-in

Invite everyone to look at the picture **In A Tree** on page 31. Give them a minute to think about how they are feeling about their place in the group right now. Do they feel they belong? Do they feel welcome and accepted? Are they excited about the direction the group is going or are they feeling unsure about its direction? Invite them to choose the person in the picture that represents how they are feeling (e.g. "I feel like the person sitting way out on the branch because I'm new this year and everyone else seems to know each other from last year").

Trusting Pairs

Try this suggestion to get the group into pairs. Have players find someone who has the same (or different)
- pet
- astrological sign
- favorite pastime
- color of hair
- number of brothers and sisters
- favorite subject/class
- favorite TV show
- favorite comic strip

Once they have a partner, have them try the following trust exercises. (You may want to get them into different pairs after each exercise. Then, for a greater challenge, have pairs find another pair and try these same exercises with four, even six people!)
- **Back-to-back** – Have partners sit back-to-back with knees bent and elbows linked. Slowly and carefully let them try to stand up together, by pushing against each other with their backs.
- **Palm-to-Palm** – Have partners stand, facing each other, and place their palms together. Each takes a step backward and then leans forward. Partners should keep each other in balance with their palms. To make this more difficult, challenge pairs to try pushing off and then falling forward against their partner's palms again, establishing a rhythm.
- **Toe-to-toe** – Have partners sit facing each other, toe-to-toe, with knees bent in front of them (toes should be touching, not overlapping). Partners hold each other's wrists or hands and pull each other up, at the same time, into a standing position.

Wind in the Willows

See the instructions for this trust game on page 32.

Needs Continuums

Label one end of the room "agree" and the other end "disagree." Imagine a line running from one end to the other.

Read out the following statements and ask everyone to position themselves on the line (i.e. at one end if strongly agreeing, at the other if strongly disagreeing, in the middle if indifferent).

1. Having a chance to socialize with my friends at youth group is important to me.
2. Having discussions about things I'm concerned about is important to me.
3. It's important to me that we have some sort of worship every week.
4. It's important to me that we do outreach projects.
5. Playing a lot of games (at youth group) is my idea of fun.
6. Youth group should be a place where people can feel comfortable talking about God, their beliefs, and questions.

Create your own statements to help you discover the different interests and needs of your group members.

Needs and Trust

What does everyone value as most important about this group? Encourage a sharing of opinions. Affirm group members' needs for all kinds of program content – social, active, and serious. When group members trust each other they express themselves honestly.

How can everyone – leaders and youth – work together to meet each other's needs? (As a leader, your feelings about the program content are valid, too.) Try the **Expectations** exercise on page 35 to encourage more thinking about the group.

Group Trust Exercises

Try these exercises to build trusting relationships.

- **Lap-Sit** – Group members stand in a circle shoulder to shoulder. Then they all turn to the left (or all to the right), take a side step into the circle, creating a smaller, tighter circle. Ask them to put their hands on the hips of the person in front of them. On a leader's count, have everyone slowly bend their knees and sit back on the lap of the person behind them. If they all work together, all will be sitting on someone's lap without any chairs! For an even greater challenge, try moving forward all at the same time – left, right, left, right.

- **Interdependence** – The group stands in a circle. Number off "one" and "two" or "in" and "out." Ask group members to hold hands, plant their feet firmly, and hold their bodies straight. On a leader's count, all the "one's" lean forward into the circle and all the "two's" lean backward, counterbalancing the "one's." For an even greater challenge, ask them to reverse themselves, alternating between leaning backwards and forwards.

- **All Aboard** – Lay a piece of fabric (or paper) on the oor. Ask group members to get on it so that everyone's feet are on it. Then ask them to step off it while you fold up several inches of the fabric, making it smaller. Ask the group to get back on. This takes a little more creativity as the space decreases for the same number of feet. Continue folding in parts of the fabric until the space is too small for the group. Then divide the group into two teams and make the fabric smaller. The team that can successfully get all its members on the fabric and hold for three seconds wins.

Closing Worship

Related Scripture Passages: Genesis 12:1-4, Hebrews 11:1-2, 8-12
Group Meditation: Pass around the picture **In a Tree** (on the next page). Ask group members to identify again their place in the group and how they feel about it. Do they feel differently about their place in the group than they did at the beginning of this gathering?

In a Tree

Wind in the Willows
A Trust Game for Four or More People

Form a circle. Ask everyone to stand tightly shoulder to shoulder, with one foot slightly behind the other for balance. Ask everyone to bend their elbows and hold their hands up at chest level with palms facing out. Now everyone imagines they are the gentle summer breeze.

Ask for a volunteer to be the "willow." The volunteer stands in the center of the circle with feet together, arms crossed over the chest, and eyes closed. Keeping feet together and body straight, the volunteer should allow their body to fall in any direction. As the "willow," the person sways from side to side, forward and backward. Those making the "breeze" support the person with gentle pushes of their palms, moving the "willow" back and forth around the circle. Encourage the "willow" to trust those in the circle to gently move them back and forth. Remind the "breeze" to take this trust and responsibility seriously. Allow everyone a chance to be the willow tree.

Use the following questions to talk about the experiences of being the "willow" and the "breeze":

- As the willow, how did it feel to put yourself in the hands of the group, some of whom you probably didn't know very well?
- Did you feel safe as the willow?
- As the breeze, how did you feel about your role?
- How did it feel to work as a group? Did you trust the rest of the group to do their part?
- How might this exercise be similar to the experiences we have as members of this group?
- How might this exercise symbolize what it means to be part of this group?

Cooperation

Group Check-in

Use a clothesline to really connect! Tie a spoon to the end of a ball of yarn. Ask a volunteer to begin by sharing one thing they did during the past week. Have them take the spoon and pass it through an item of clothing they are wearing (e.g. down the neck of their shirt and out the sleeve). Then have them pass the spoon to someone else. That person shares something and strings the yarn through their clothes, too. Eventually the whole group will be on the clothesline together. Have them do something all together (e.g. walk from one end of the room to the other) before you take them off the line.

Cooperative Relay

Divide the group into two teams. Design a relay course that teams have to travel through together. Team members help one another. Assign points for teams that successfully get all members through and take away points for mistrials.

- **Hoop of Fire** – Using rope, suspend a hoop about 4 feet (1.5m) off the ground in a doorway. Teams must work together to get members through the "hoop of fire" without them touching the hoop.

- **Live Wires** – String a rope between two poles or pillars about 5 feet (1.75cm) from the ground. Provide the youth with a chair and a 1 ft. x 1 ft. (30 x 30cm) plywood board about 1/2 in. (1.25cm) thickness. With these, teams must get members over (not under) the power line without touching it.

- **Suspension Bridge** – Holding hands, teams must get onto, across, and off a balance beam together without losing balance.

- **Lava Flow** – (This requires an uncarpeted oor space.) Using two chairs, teams must get all members from one end of the room to the other.

Disaster Scene Simulation

You will need: two or three blindfolds, slips of paper with descriptions of different injuries (e.g. unconscious, completely paralyzed, unable to see, unable to move left leg, right arm broken, paralyzed from waist down).

Instructions: Explain to the youth that a disaster has just occurred (e.g. a train wreck, gas explosion). They are all injured and will have to travel – either alone or with someone else – to the hospital (a designated spot as far from the "victims" as possible). Give each group member a piece of paper that describes their injury. Each person reads their own slip of paper and immediately assumes the condition. For example, someone "unconscious" lies down. They do not tell others their injury. (*Note:* The leader does not participate, but observes, to ensure group members' safety in the exercise.)

After group members have all reached the "hospital" talk about the experience. How did you feel about your role? Were you able to work as a group or was it "everyone for themselves"? Which role would have been hardest for you? Why? What did you learn about yourself during this exercise? What did you learn about being "community" and the importance of cooperating?

Island in the Sun

You will need: newsprint sheets, masking tape, "island" music, and tape player

Instructions: Tape 4 or 5 pieces of newsprint to the oor. Have everyone choose an "island" on which to "sun" themselves. Play some reggae or other Caribbean music. Encourage people to go cruising around and visit other islands. (If you want to go all out bring sunglasses and sun hats for people to wear.) While they are wandering around and greeting each other, remove one of the islands. When the music stops they must all find an island so they don't drown. Continue this process, removing one island each time, until everyone is together "sunning" on the same island. They may need to support one another so no one falls off and drowns.

We were created to live in community and support one another. What might this exercise symbolize about "being in community"? What challenges do you think we face as a group? How will we ensure that everyone feels a part of this community?

Tug of Peace

Tie the ends of a tug-of-war rope together. Ask group members to sit in a circle on their knees and hold the rope with two hands (hands resting on knees). Move back to widen the circle if necessary, until the rope becomes slightly taut. On your word the group begins to pull on the rope, exerting an even pressure around the circle until the rope becomes quite taut. Continue pulling, until the tension on the rope pulls everyone up on their feet!

Cooperating in Community

- Discuss what it means to be a community.
- Based on this discussion, establish some group "norms" or standards for behavior that promote trust. Ask for suggestions and incorporate these into a statement. You might want to write these on the "island" the group ended up on (see **Island in the Sun** on this page). Post this statement where it will be visible throughout the year.
- If you created norms or standards in a previous week, review these today. Ask the group to evaluate how well the standards have been maintained. Use **Community Links** (below) to help.

Community Links

Hand out strips of construction paper and markers. Give group members a couple of minutes to write the following on opposite sides of the strip:

1. One thing they like about the group or that the group has done together, and
2. One thing they haven't enjoyed or liked about the group so far.

Have them attach their strips using tape or a stapler to create a chain. Use the final strip to connect the two ends of the chain. Stand in a circle (inside and outside the chain) and have everyone take hold of a link that is not their own. One at a time, have group members read out what is written on both sides of the link. There is no need for group members to identify the one they wrote.

Closing Worship

Related Scripture Passages: Mark 9:33-35, Colossians 3:12-14

Collage Prayer: Ask group members to look through some newspapers and magazines and tear out pictures, headlines, and words that reflect something that concerns them. When everyone is ready, gather in a circle around a large sheet of newsprint. Invite everyone to add silently their picture or clipping to the newsprint, creating a prayer collage. Together and silently, look at the things others have added to the collage and reflect on these concerns.

Idea Page #5　Communication

Group Check-in

We don't always use words to communicate with others. Sometimes we use body language. Explain that for this check-in everyone is invited to "strike a pose" that expresses how they are feeling right now. On the leader's count, group members strike a pose and hold it. Give each person a chance to look around the room and notice (without explaining or discussing) how others are standing. Ask them to take a minute to think about this. For example, if they notice someone looking tired or anxious, how might this affect the way they approach or interact with that person?

Expectations

Help group members understand that people other than themselves have expectations of this group. Divide the group into several teams and give each a premise. Ask each team to create and then share a short conversation about this premise.

Premise #1
Two parents of youth group members explain to two parents who are new to the congregation the benefits of their teens attending the young people's group.

Premise #2
Two members of the youth group explain to a friend why they participate and what they do. They each come for different reasons.

Premise #3
One minister explains to another the merits and contents of their youth ministry program.

After the teams have presented their conversations, discuss the importance of the group for all these people. How can this youth group recognize the different expectations?

Reprinted from *Seeds & Sowers for Youth Ministry*, Volume 14, Division of Mission in Canada. © The United Church of Canada, Etobicoke, Canada. Reprinted by permission.

Framed!

You will need: several cartoon strips with three or more frames (cut apart individual frames), safety pins

Instructions: Hand a cartoon frame and safety pin to each member of the group and ask them to pin these onto the front of their shirts. Explain that they must not talk while they complete the rest of the exercise. Give them one minute to find all the others with frames of the same cartoon and get into order (i.e. put the frames in order).

Picture This

Ask group members to find a partner and sit back-to-back with them. Hand one partner a blank piece of paper and a marker. Give the other a pre-drawn picture (e.g. of a simple house, clouds in the sky and birds). Instruct them not to show this to their partner. Invite them to describe the picture carefully to their partner so that their partner can draw a copy of it. They must not tell their partner what the object is they are describing. They can only give instructions like "Draw a square. Draw a triangle above the square, but touching the square."

After the activity, invite partners to compare the pictures. Discuss how it felt to try to explain the drawing or to figure out what the other person meant. What was frustrating about the experience?

Stampede

Explain that you will read out a series of instructions that all begin with "Touch someone who..." and a description. Ask everyone to follow the instructions and find someone who fits that description, placing a hand gently on that person.

Below are some examples. You might want to tailor these for your group; add a few descriptions that perhaps would fit only one or two people in your group and then stand clear of the stampede!

Example: "Touch someone who..."

...has blue eyes

...is wearing running shoes

...is wearing an earring

...is wearing glasses

...was born in October

...has a name that begins with the letter "S"

Traffic Jam

See the instructions on page 37 for this game.

Activities for the year

What does everyone expect from this group this year? Record the different expectations on newsprint. Using these ideas, do some long-range planning. Include participation in worship services, retreats and service projects. Plan ways to raise money if needed. What other support will you require for the other activities you're planning? How will you go about acquiring this?

Non-Verbal Game

Play a game like Pictionary™ or Charades if someone can bring one of them from home. These games encourage different ways of communicating ideas.

Survival

Hand out copies of **Survival Game** on page 38. Read the instructions and play the game. Afterwards, in the total group, discuss the following questions:

- What influenced you when you made individual choices?
- What influenced you when you made group choices?
- What values do your choices reflect?

Group Communication

Communication is really important for creating and maintaining healthy relationships between people. Reflect on the communication in your group: Who asks questions? Who answers questions? Who jokes? Who is silent? and so on. Take time to discuss challenges encountered as a group. Invite youth to talk about what's frustrating about not being listened to, concerns about group members who are shy and don't get a chance to talk, what it feels like if contributions aren't respected. What other concerns do they have?

Signing Good-Bye

Closing Worship

Related Scripture Passages: Proverbs 15:1-4, Proverbs 26:17-23, John 18:28-38

Ritual: Use one of the following non-verbal rituals for your closing or create your own.

1. **Group Hug:** Everyone stands in a circle, holding hands. Then with hands still held, lift them overhead and step forward, lowering them behind. Everyone should then be standing very close for a mighty HUG.

2. **Signing Good-Bye:** Our modern English "good-bye" is actually a shortened version of "God be with you." Learn the signs (from American Sign Language) for this phrase and practice these a few times. Then form two circles, one inside the other. The inside circle faces group members standing in the outside circle. Invite them to make the sign "God be with you" to their partner. Then the outside circle moves once to the left and repeats until everyone has had a chance to wish each other "good-bye."

Traffic Jam

Count out eight sheets of newsprint and draw one arrow on each. Arrange these on the floor with one blank sheet of newsprint in the center (as shown in Step 1 of the solution below). Ask group members to stand on the papers, facing the direction indicated by the arrow. No one should stand on the blank paper. (If you have fewer than four in the group, members can move objects such as shoes on the arrows instead. With groups larger than eight, create a second "traffic jam.")

The object of the game is to have the two groups of people (on the left of the blank square and on the right of the blank square) exchange places, still facing in the original direction.

The following moves are **legal**:
- You may move into an empty space in front of you.
- You may move around another who is facing you into an empty space.

The following moves are **illegal**:
- You may not move backwards.
- You may not move around another who is facing your same direction into an empty space.
- Two people cannot move at the same time.

Here is the solution:

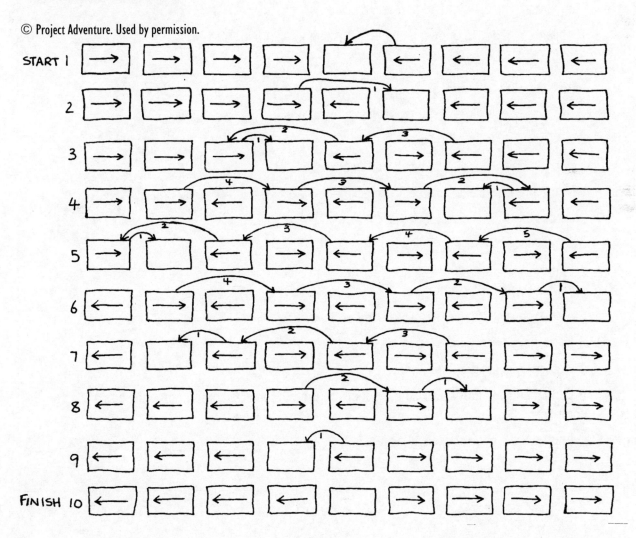

Survival Game

Instructions: Together read over "The Situation" in the box.
Allow group members a few minutes to do this individually.
Then divide into groups of four and repeat the process,
deciding as a group which eight items they will take.
They have five minutes to decide.

The Situation

There is an impending, catastrophic disaster expected to occur in the very near future so that life as we know it may come to an end. You have been chosen to be part of a select group of persons who are going to travel to a remote place in order to start a new community and continue civilization. Some things you would like to take with you are listed below. You may take only eight items. Put a check mark beside the eight items in the following list that you think are the most important to take with you.

The List

__ A variety of seeds for fruits and vegetables

__ Dehydrated fruits, nuts, and preserves

__ A collection of books of poems, novels, biographies and short stories

__ Several animals of your choice

__ Medicines and a first-aid kit

__ Some basic tools like hammers, saws, shovels, hoes, axes, etc.

__ Sewing materials and fabrics

__ Binoculars, telescope, microscope and compass

__ Some other books like a medical encyclopedia, farming and construction

manuals, cook books, nature books

__ the Bible

__ A battery-operated radio and tape recorder with a collection of 50 selected tape recordings and also some blank tapes

__ Several musical instruments and books of music

__ Pots, pans, cooking utensils, candles, rope

__ A water purifying/filtration system

__ Personal hygiene items including a supply of anti-bacterial soap, toothbrush & paste, hair comb, etc.

__ One other item of your choice. What is it? _____

Hunger

Group Check-in

This is a "thumbs up" exercise! Without discussing or explaining, invite everyone to express how they are feeling by giving a thumbs up, thumbs down, or indicating "in-between." Ask group members to look around and notice how others are feeling.
Encourage them to be sensitive to this as they interact during their time together.

Let's Go Shopping

Divide into small groups of three or four. Ask each group to plan a menu for a week for a family of three – a single mother and two children. The family has a stove, oven and refrigerator. After paying their rent, they have $58 per week to spend on groceries. Provide flyers from local grocery stores. Ask the groups to create a grocery list (with prices). When finished, ask everyone to come together and share the results. Consider the following questions:

- Was the group able to stay within its budget?
- Have any ingredients been missed?
- Are there any items on the grocery list that seem like non-essentials?
- Is this menu nutritionally well balanced?
- As you planned the menu, did the group decide it couldn't afford some items? Which ones?

Ask everyone to return to the original small groups. Explain that, because the weather has become colder, the family has had to pay $12 more for the heating bill this month. They now have only $46 to spend on groceries. Ask the groups to look at their menus and grocery lists. What can they eliminate? Return to the larger group and discuss their ideas using the same questions. Talk about what other options a family in this situation would have (e.g. go to a food bank, find cheaper accommodation).

40 Hour Fast

See page 116 for information and suggestions on holding your own 40-hour fast. Plan a fast for whatever time period is appropriate for your group.

Hunger Stories

Read some Bible stories about hunger. Divide into small groups and assign each group a different passage: Exodus 16:1-21, Ruth 1:1-6, Matthew 15:32-38, Luke 15: 11-24. Have them read the stories together, discussing the following questions: Who in this story was hungry? What was the cause of their hunger? How did they respond to the situation they found themselves in? How did others respond? How did God respond?

Ask the groups to create a modern version of the story. Have them present these in written or dramatic form to the rest of the group.

Why are People Hungry?

Together brainstorm the causes of hunger in the world today. How do people respond to hungry people? How do you think God responds? How do you think we are called to respond?

Food Bank or Shelter Tour

Contact churches or organizations that provide services for homeless people, runaways, or others in need.

If it's appropriate, ask to have a tour and have someone speak to the group about the work the organization does. (If this is not appropriate, ask about other possibilities. Some organizations will be able to provide you with an informative video or send a speaker.)

Be sure to allow enough time to debrief afterwards. As a group, plan a fund-raising project to support this organization.

Food Bank Trick-or-Treat

Plan to wear costumes and go trick-or-treating for donations to the local food bank this Halloween! Contact the food bank ahead of time. Work with them to create a card with a simple message to give to people who donate food. It might thank them and give a brief description of the local food bank (e.g. where it's located, how many people it serves, what it needs). Include the signature of the food bank's director as you may need to prove you are soliciting on behalf of the food bank.

Divide the group into several teams and give each a cardboard box (or potato sack or old pillowcase). You may need to arrange for a vehicle or some other mid-way drop-off point for teams. When you visit people's homes, be sure to explain that you are a church youth group and that instead of collecting candy you're collecting non-perishable food items for the food bank. Leave a card and thank them for their support.

Be sure to have a picture taken of everyone with all the food they collect. You might even want to contact a local newspaper or TV station ahead of time to see if they're interested in covering the story. This gives the local food bank some free publicity.

Hunger Awareness Meal

Plan a hunger awareness meal. Here's what one group did:

The youth group sold tickets to the dinner ahead of time ($8 per family). As people arrived, they drew a card out of a hat. One quarter of the cards said "Developed Country (First World)." Three quarters of the cards said "Developing Country (Third World)."

The room was divided to give the largest area to people from the First World. The area was set with tables, tablecloths, candles, flowers, etc. Waiters served a full-course meal. The people from the Developing Countries came to the kitchen pass-through window for a bowl of broth with a few vegetables. They sat on the floor. Afterward they talked about their experiences.

The youth had donated all the food. They donated the money raised to their church's mission fund.

Slide Prayers

Create a short slide (or video) show that could be used as a prayer in a worship about hunger.

Plan to spend a few hours together one afternoon taking pictures. Photograph organizations in your community that work with people in need (e.g. at a food bank, shelter, drop-in center), or of other things that symbolize concerns the group has about their community and world (e.g. the local dump). If you are interested, set these to music. The images themselves will be powerful and thought-provoking.

Closing Worship

Related Scripture Passages: Matthew 25:34-40, Luke 6:21a, Revelation 7:16-17
Story: Read the modern parable **King and Queen of All the Land** on the following pages.
Prayer: Creator God, help us to remember that it is you who have provided us with the abundance of resources we so often refer to as "ours." Help us to see that you have provided enough for all, if only we would share. Help us realize that people have less than we do because we have more than we need. Amen.

King and Queen of All the Land
(A Modern Parable)

Once there was a King and Queen who led the people with fairness and care. The land was never at war and there were never any poor or hungry. Everyone had what they needed, but not too much. All the people were happy.

But the King and Queen were getting old, and knew it was time to choose their successors. They put up signs throughout the land:

Wanted! A New Queen and King.

Must be strong, firm, fair, wise, kind and trustworthy.

They received lots of applications and they found three couples that seemed quite suitable. Barth and Elizabeth were strong, loyal, just, and brave, and had helped the army make peace several times. Xtapa (Ex-TA-pa) and Iquizal (EYE-quee-zal) were honest, loyal, and reliable, with lots of past experience, having been king and queen of another kingdom. Cleopath and Zanzumble were noble, true, and caring, and came with excellent references.

"These seem like very fine potential leaders," said the King. "It is so difficult to decide."

"We should devise a test," said the Queen. The King agreed and the three couples were summoned. When everyone was there, the King and Queen handed each couple a loaf of freshly baked bread. It was crusty on the outside, still warm, and smelled delicious.

"You must care for this loaf as you would the whole land," said the Queen. "Tomorrow morning when you return we shall see how you have done."

"This test is so easy it's laughable," said Barth and Elizabeth. They saddled their horses and galloped off down the road. They kept their swords ready to defend the bread, but never needed them. The only people they passed were an old beggar and a woman carrying a child who was crying.

Xtapa and Iquizal knew from experience in their previous kingdom that fresh smelling bread is tempting. When people are hungry they will do almost anything to get some food. Xtapa and Iquizal decided to keep it safe in a heavy vault, with 16 padlocks and 50 steel chains. They stayed awake all night guarding the vault, but needn't have worried. The only person who came by was an old man in rags. He smelled the bread and begged them to give him some, but he was so frail that he posed no threat. Later that night they saw a woman carrying a child. The child was sobbing and asking for something to eat, but the woman passed by and they didn't have to worry about her trying to steal from them.

Cleopath and Zanzumble put the bread into a basket and set off. An old man hobbled down the roads towards them.

"Greetings to you," croaked the old man. "That fresh bread you are carrying smells delicious. May I have a bite, for I haven't eaten all day."

Cleopath and Zanzumble hesitated. "We're supposed to be protecting this

(continued on next page)

King and Queen of All the Land *(continued)*

bread for the King and Queen," they replied.

"Surely they wouldn't want an old man to go hungry," said the old man. Cleopath and Zanzumble looked at each other, knowing this could mean they would fail the test.

"This old man really needs something to eat," said Zanzumble. So they gave the old man a big chunk of bread. He thanked them and departed.

A few minutes later they saw a woman carrying a child. The child was wailing.

"Hush, little one," murmured the woman, "I have nothing to give you." Hearing this, Cleopath and Zanzumble also offered them a large chunk of the bread. They thanked Cleopath and Zanzumble and went on their way. During the rest of the day Cleopath and Zanzumble met others in need. They kept sharing the bread until the whole loaf was gone.

The next morning, Cleopath and Zanzumble headed back, feeling a little sad that they wouldn't be chosen as the new King and Queen. Xtapa and Iquizal galloped passed them on the road and saw that they carried nothing.

"They have certainly failed the test," said Xtapa smugly. "See, they have lost the loaf."

A few minutes later Barth and Elizabeth strode by, carrying the heavy box still wrapped in chains. They saw that Cleopath and Zanzumble carried nothing with them. "We'll surely win," they said gleefully. "Our bread is still secure."

The King and Queen gathered the three couples together and asked them how they had fared. "We galloped all night," said Barth and Elizabeth, "and here's our bread, that we cared for so well." The bread was a little squashed from all the hard riding, but the King and Queen didn't seem to notice.

"Here is our bread," said Xtapa and Iquizal, opening the 16 padlocks and undoing the 50 steel chains. They pulled out the loaf. It was a little stale and hard, but again the King and Queen said nothing.

Cleopath and Zanzumble lowered their heads. "We're sorry that we're not able to return your loaf," they said, "We met some hungry people on the road, and we gave them the bread. We have failed your test." Hearing this, the King and Queen smiled.

"Cleopath and Zanzumble, you have passed the test!" they said. "The old couple that you helped was us in disguise. We saw that you cared for the bread as you would care for all the land, with love and generosity. You cared more for the people you met than for passing the test. You are worthy to be our successors. We hereby appoint you the new King and Queen of All the Land."

Idea Page #7

Halloween and All Saints' Day

Group Check-in

Choose a monster that describes how you are feeling right now. Take turns explaining your choice to the other group members (e.g. "Right now I am feeling like the Loch Ness Monster because people don't really know who I am").

Planning a Halloween Party

- Invite everyone to come dressed as their favorite saint. (They may need to do a little research first.)
- Have a bonfire and roast hot dogs and apples or try the recipes below to make **Halloween Drinks**. Encourage group members to bring friends.
- Plan to have the closing worship outdoors if weather permits.
- Use the ideas on these pages to plan a program of games, crafts, and closing worship.

Halloween Drinks

Witch's Brew

1 can concentrated orange juice
same amount water
1 qt. (1 L) white grape juice
5 drops green food coloring
2 qts. (2 L) carbonated lemon-lime soda pop
washed plastic spiders, crawlies

Put everything except plastic crawlies and soda in a large punch bowl. Dump 2 trays of ice cubes in the bowl. Float washed plastic crawlies on top of the punch. *To serve:* Add the lemon-lime soda and watch the concoction begin to fizz and bubble, bouncing the spiders and crawlies in and out of this ghastly brew!

Hot Spiced Apple Drink

4 qts.(4 L) apple juice
2/3 cup (160 ml) brown sugar
3 cinnamon sticks
5 whole cloves
fresh orange slices

Pour juice into a Dutch oven or large pot. Dissolve brown sugar into juice. Add sliced oranges, cloves, and cinnamon sticks. Bring to a boil. Simmer on low heat for 30 minutes.

Food Bank Trick-or-Treat

See page 40 for a description of this community service project.

Who Am I?

Instructions: Print the names of well-known saints and martyrs on pieces of paper. Tape one paper to the back of each player. Explain that the objective is to try to guess the name on your back by asking other players questions that can be answered only with a "yes" or "no" (e.g. Am I female?). Everyone mills around and can ask each person one question. If some people need more help, invite the group to give some more clues.

All Saints' Day Game

Try this variation of "Upset the Apple Cart."
Instructions: Assign group members the names of well-known saints, making sure that each name is used more than once. Arrange chairs (one fewer than the number of players you have) in a circle and have a volunteer be "the caller." The caller stands in the center of the circle while the others sit on chairs. The caller calls out a saint's name (e.g. "St. Patrick!") and all players who have been given that name get up and exchange seats with another "St. Patrick." The caller also tries to claim a seat. The one left without a seat becomes the new caller. Occasionally the caller may shout "All Saints Day!" Then everyone must get up and claim a new seat. Here are some saints' names you might use: Patrick, Nicholas, Mary Magdalene, Peter, Cecilia, Valentine.

Paper Bag Luminaries

You will need: paper lunch sacks, sharpened pencils, hole punches, votive candles, sand or gravel

Instructions: Hand out paper bags. Invite everyone to create a design on theirs that expresses something about their inner selves. They may wish to draw this design with a pencil first. Then, using a hole punch or sharpened tip of a pencil, carefully punch holes in the bag following the design. Place about 1/2 in. (1cm) of sand or gravel in the bottom of the bags. Light votive candles and carefully place these in the bottom (center) of the bags. Turn out the lights and enjoy the effect. (Note: Small votive candles or tea lights do not give off enough heat to cause a fire. If the top of the bag is left open any heat will escape that way. However, do not leave these bags unattended.)

Rolled Beeswax Candles

You will need: sheets of honeycomb wax, wicking, sharp art knife. Sheets of beeswax are 16 1/2 in. x 8 1/2 in. (41cm x 22cm) and cost $2-$3 per sheet. Each sheet makes 2 candles.

Instructions: On each wax sheet, mark 7 in. (18cm) from each end at the bottom left and top right. Cut diagonally from one mark to the other. Hang a 10 in. (25cm) piece of wicking down the long 9 1/2 in. (24cm) side, pressing it into the wax. Roll wax and wicking into a tight roll to form a candle.

(Also see instructions for **Dipped Candles** on page 50.)

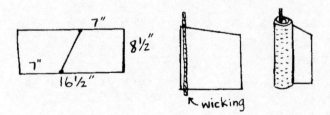

Movie Posters

Hand out sheets of newsprint and markers. Ask everyone to imagine for a moment that a movie is being made about their lives. The biographer is particularly interested in their spiritual life, and how their beliefs in God have affected their life direction and choices.

Allow them a few minutes to imagine what the movie might portray. Explain that their piece of newsprint will be like a movie poster. On the sheet of newsprint, have them write a title for the movie and draw a picture if they wish. This could be of a scene of significance in their lives. Then, at the bottom of the page, have them write the names of some of the people who have "starred" in their lives. Who are some of the people who have been important role models? Who have encouraged and influenced them on their faith journey?

Tape the posters up around the room and invite group members to go and look at the other posters.

Communion of Saints

We are Christians today because Christians down through the centuries passed on their faith from one generation to the next. We call this line or "community" of faithful people "the Communion of Saints." All Saints' Day is a time to remember those who have influenced our lives and guided us in our faith. How has the Christian faith been passed on over the centuries? How was it passed on to you or how is it being passed on to you?

We are also part of the Communion of Saints. When we describe saints as being "holy," we don't necessarily mean someone who is "perfect" or a hero. The word "holy" means set apart. Each of us, in our own way, is set apart for God's purposes. How do we pass on our faith? To whom are we passing it?

Closing Worship

Related Scripture Passage: Revelation 7:9-17
Litany Prayer: See the next page for the prayer **I Will Be with You Always.**
Meditation: Read **Stained Glass Lives** on page 47.

I Will Be with You Always
(Matthew 28:20)

In Central America, and a growing number of places throughout the world, the names of the dead, saints and martyrs are read out in church or at gatherings such as peace and human rights demonstrations. The names of those who have "gone before" – those who are missing (prisoners of conscience), influential religious and political leaders and "common people" who have given their lives for their convictions – are honored and remembered in the reading of their names. The people listening respond "PRESENTE!" (pronounced press-EN-tay). This means "present" or "here." It is like calling the roll of those who belong to the community that is struggling for peace and justice in God's world.

In this way those gathered express their belief that even though these people are not physically present, their presence is still among them in a powerful way. This is what the church means when it talks about the communion or community of saints.
(Light the central candle. Set out 13 smaller candles. Each time the leader speaks, light a candle from the central one.)

Prayer: O God, we gather before you in prayer
remembering the many who have given their lives
working for justice and peace for all peoples.
May we, in this moment of thanksgiving and
yearning for Shalom,
be strengthened and renewed
by their example and presence
and by your Spirit in our midst.
We remember in love:

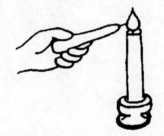

Leader: Steven Biko, black activist who died while in detention, in South Africa, September 12, 1977.

All: Presente!

Leader: The 40,000 martyrs in the struggle for the liberation of Nicaragua.

All: Presente!

Leader: The native martyrs of the Ixil and Quiché people burned alive in the Spanish Embassy in Guatemala on January 31, 1980.

All: Presente!

Leader: Archbishop Oscar Romero, assassinated by the death squad while saying the Mass, March 24, 1980 in El Salvador.

All: Presente!

Leader: The four American church women: Jean Donovan and Sisters Ita Ford, Maura Clarke and Dorothy Kazel, raped and murdered by the death squad in El Salvador, December 3, 1980.

(continued on next page)

I Will Be with You Always *(continued)*

All: Presente!

Leader: The 75,000 dead, 7,000 disappeared and 1.5 million internal refugees in El Salvador.

All: Presente!

Leader: Those imprisoned in the United States for harboring refugees from the violence in Central America.

All: Presente!

Leader: Those killed in Tiananmen Square, Beijing, June 3, 1989.

All: Presente!

Leader: Six Jesuit priests – Ignacio Martin-Baro, Segundo Montes, Ignacio Ellacuria, Juan Ramon Moreno, Amando Lopez, and Joaquin Lopez y Lopez – and their housekeeper Julia Elba Ramon and her daughter Celina, all murdered by the death squad, November 16, 1989, at the University of Central America, San Salvador.

All: Presente!

Leader: Fourteen women engineering students killed at the University of Montreal, December 6, 1989.

All: Presente!

Leader: Those who died during the Gulf War, and those who are now homeless, destitute, hungry or ill due to the destruction of war.

All: Presente!

Leader: Ryan White, a hemophiliac who contracted AIDS through blood transfusions and died April 8, 1990, and all those who have died from the disease.

All: Presente!

Leader: All those whom we know personally, and name now in silence, who have suffered for their convictions or whose lives have inspired us and revealed God to us. (Allow time for silent prayers. Invite any who want to, to share their prayers out loud.)

All: Presente!

Stained Glass Lives

Lessons from two different kinds of light.

For centuries, stained glass was seen mostly in churches. It lent a special aura to the interiors of church buildings, the colored light splashing over pews and columns, floors and woodwork.

Lately, however, stained glass has become popular in bars and restaurants. Not with religious subjects, of course. You're more likely to see bunches of purple grapes hanging from pea-green vines, or barns backed by mellow maples.

In one such restaurant, the fluorescent lights behind the glass had gone out. And I realized that the stained glass scene, as art, was awful. It only looked good because of the light shining through it. I suspect that's true of most stained glass – though some artists work only with glass, and produce true works of art. But if most stained glass windows were painted onto our walls, we'd reject them. Anyone offering stained-glass wall paper would go broke. And if someone splashed colored paint over our church pews and floors, we'd call them a vandal.

It's the light shining through the glass that makes the difference. It works differently in our brains. Reflected light – the light that bounces off paper or walls or paintings – usually gets processed by the left hemisphere of our brains. The left hemisphere is critical, analytical, intellectual. Transmitted light, on the other hand, works with the right side of our brains. We suspend critical judgment. It gets us involved.

The moral of this story? It's simple. When we try to persuade people intellectually, they will inevitably react in a left-brain manner, analyzing critically our message. But when we live our beliefs – in a sense, letting the light shine *through* us – they're more likely to get personally involved.

by James Taylor, March, 1980, from Currents, Volume 5, No. 2. Used by permission.

Peace and Remembrance

Group Check-in

Play **Back from the World**. Print the following on a sheet of newsprint: "Hello, I'm _____ and I've been out in the world. I could tell you one thing I've _____." Invite someone to begin by reading the sentence, inserting one of the "sense" words (e.g. seen, smelled, heard, felt, learned, experienced). Then the rest of the group responds: "Welcome _____, back from the world. Tell us what you _____" (e.g. saw, smelled, heard, felt, learned, experienced). Then the group member shares something that's happened in their life recently. Continue until everyone has had a chance to share something.

Peace Symbols

You need: sheets of newsprint for everyone, scissors, glue, and magazines.

Instructions: At the top of the sheet of newsprint ask everyone to write "This picture symbolizes peace to me because..." Then invite them to take a few minutes to look through the magazines and choose a picture that represents "peace" to them. Ask them to cut this out, glue it to their page, and write below it a sentence describing why they chose that picture.

Place the sheets in a circle on the floor. Give everyone a marker and have them move one space to their left (so that they are standing in front of someone else's picture). Invite them to look at the picture and read what the person has written. Then invite them to add a comment to the page about how the picture makes them feel or what it symbolizes for them. Continue moving around the circle until everyone has returned to their own page. Give them a minute to read the comments others have written.

Remembering the Holocaust

Plan to visit a local synagogue or Jewish community center just prior to November (Holocaust Month). Check to see what upcoming special events or services are open to the public. Or view a film about anti-Semitism. Read aloud **The Anniversary of Kristallnacht** on page 52.

War Memorial Visit

Plan to visit a local war memorial or a nearby cemetery where victims of war are buried. On slips of paper, write prayers of concern for people in countries where there is war or unrest, and for people serving overseas – UN peacekeepers, chaplains, enlisted personnel. Incorporate these into the worship.

Armed Forces Guest Speaker

Invite a retired or active military chaplain to talk about their role in the armed forces. This is an excellent chance for young people to hear about "non-militaristic" aspects of the armed forces. Our perceptions of the military may be challenged!

Write a Peacekeeper

Consider writing some notes or cards to enlisted personnel serving overseas, especially those on peacekeeping missions. They are often separated from their families for long periods of time and will enjoy hearing from you. Include a picture of the group, some drawings, or clippings from a local newspaper. Send these through the chaplain services of the armed forces.

Dipped Candles

It takes 5-10 minutes to make a candle. It's best to have 1-3 people working together at a "station."

You will need:

- two 48 oz. (1.5 L) juice cans – one filled with cold water, the other for the wax
- large pot (to boil water in) – it must be tall enough to hold juice cans for melting wax. Water should go at least half-way up the side of the cans
- newspapers
- paraffin wax – 1 lb. (500g) will make about 6 large candles but you'll need more volume for dipping into. Start with 2 lbs. (1 kg) and add wax for number of candles you wish to make
- candle wicking (10 in. (25cm) for each candle)
- candle dye or old broken wax crayons (papers removed) for color if desired
- masking tape and pen
- stove

Instructions: Start at least one hour before the candles are needed. Cover work area with newspapers. Put water in pot and put on stove to heat. Put wax in juice cans and put into pot to melt. (Hint: Wax melts quicker when it is broken up into small pieces first.) Add crayons or candle dye for color if desired. Put cold water in the second juice can on the oor. Put can of melted wax on the oor next to the can with cold water in it. Hold wick at one end and dip all but 1 inch into hot wax, being careful not to touch it. Then dip wick into cold water tin. As you pull it out, smooth the cooled wax through your thumb and first finger in a downward pulling motion. (Note: Do this after each dip to make your candle smooth and straight.) Dip the wick into the hot wax a second time and remove quickly, placing it in the cold water. Make sure your dips are quick or the heat will re-melt what you have already accumulated. Use masking tape and pen to label completed candles.

See also **Rolled Beeswax Candles** on page 44, **Paper Bag Luminaries** on page 44, and **Tin Can Luminaries** on page 77.

Dietrich Bonhoeffer – Risk-Taker

Read the box below about Dietrich Bonhoeffer. Use excerpts from one of the collections of his writings for part of your program.

> ### Did you know?
> During W.W.II, many Christians protested against the persecution of Jews. Some risked their lives and safety by hiding Jews in their homes or taking part in the underground resistance to Nazism. Dietrich Bonhoeffer, a German Christian, was one such person. He was imprisoned and later executed for his role in an attempted assassination of Hitler. Some of the things he wrote while in prison are available in collections like *Bonhoeffer for a New Generation,* ed. Otto Dudzus, SCM Press, 1986 and *The Martyred Christian: 160 Readings from Dietrich Bonhoeffer,* ed. Joan Winmill Brown, Macmillan Publishing Co., 1983.

Closing Worship

Related Scripture Passage: Isaiah 2:4-5
Prayer Litany: Use the **Candle Lighting Litany for Peace** on the next page.
If you made candles, use them for this worship.

Candle Lighting Litany for Peace

Begin with an unlit candle in the center of the circle symbolizing Christ's presence.

Reader #1: O God, our world is filled with war and hatred, intolerance and ignorance. Into this world you have sent your son Jesus, the light of the world, to show us a new way. *(Light the Christ candle.)*

All: God, help us to reflect that light to others.

Reader #2: Like the crowds that followed you, sometimes we, too, are followers – not leaders. We participate in the intolerance rather than accepting others. But you have sent your son Jesus to be our example, to help us understand that your love is for everyone. *(Light a candle from the Christ candle.)*

All: God, give us courage to stand apart from the crowd – to be leaders for peace and reconciliation.

Reader #3: O God, we acknowledge that, as a human race, we have too often let our differences divide us. We've let ignorance and pride cloud our perceptions. Into this human race, you have sent your son Jesus to challenge us to see each other in new ways. *(Light a candle from the Christ candle.)*

All: God, give us the wisdom to see our differences as our strengths.

Reader #4: O God, we lift up to you in prayer the places in our world, our countries and communities, where racial, political and religious intolerance has caused violence and fear. *(Allow time for silent prayer or invite youth to offer prayers about places or things in the world that concern them.)*

Reader #5: We light these candles in remembrance of those who have died. *(Invite the youth to take a candle and light it from the Christ candle, saying the name – out loud if they wish – of someone who has died that they want to remember. This can be someone they were close to, a political leader who was assassinated or other public figure who has died.)*

Reader #6: We light these candles as a symbol of our own commitment to peace.

All: God, give us strength to carry your light within us into the world. Amen.

The Anniversary of *Kristallnacht*

In 1938, 17,000 Jews of Polish origin were expelled from Germany and dumped in a small town across the Polish border. At first, Polish authorities refused to accept them, and they were forced to live for weeks in filthy, manure-covered stables until Poland changed its mind.

Herschel Grynszpan, a 17-year-old boy, was angry and distraught upon learning that his parents were among those who had been expelled. On November 7 he shot and killed a minor official at the German embassy in Paris. This was the excuse the German Nazis had been looking for to unleash a deadly "pogrom" (massacre) against the Jewish population. Nazi regional chiefs were instructed to destroy Jewish shops, synagogues, businesses, and homes. On the evening of November 9, soldiers of the German army, in plain clothes and armed with crowbars, axes, and fire-bombs, set fire to at least 1,118 synagogues. They looted and destroyed hundreds of Jewish-owned stores and homes. More than 1,000 Jews were killed and 30,000 others were arrested and sent to concentration camps. The night became known as *Kristallnacht* (Crystal Night), or "The Night of the Broken Glass" because the streets of so many German cities were strewn with the broken glass from the windows and storefronts of Jewish homes and businesses.

Hitler had been hesitant to sanction such violence as this before then because he was fearful of opposition from the German population and from the world. Having recently returned from Munich where he had intimidated the major powers, he grew bolder. It is said that Hitler believed that "if the German people could stomach Kristallnacht, they could swallow anything." Following Kristallnacht, law after law was passed limiting the freedom of Jewish people, forbidding them to own valuables, buy rationed food, go to school, or own businesses. In September 1941, a law was passed stating that "all Jews from the age of six are forbidden to appear in public without displaying the Jewish star." The "Final Solution," the Nazi plan to "liquidate" all Jews in Europe, began the same year.

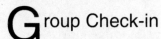 **Idea Page #9**

Leadership

Group Check-in

Invite everyone to complete the following sentence (beginning with "My name is...," if necessary): "I come to youth group because..." (e.g. "I come to youth group because it's a place where I can be myself"). What are the main reasons for being in this group?

Leadership Qualities

You will need: Letter-size sheets of paper, 12 pens, and 2 x 2 in. (5 x 5cm) cards (12 per person).

Instructions: Hand out the cards and paper. Ask everyone to fold the paper into 12 squares and number the squares from 1-12. Ask them to prioritize the list of qualities (below) that they think a leader should have from #1 (most important) to #12 (least important). Slowly read the list, allowing time between each one for youth to write the quality down on one of their cards and put it in one of the squares. Explain that they may reposition their cards as they go along.

List of Leadership Qualities
a) good listener
b) honest, trustworthy
c) questioner and challenger
d) popular
e) believes in the equality of all people
f) supports others
g) good physical appearance
h) believes in God
i) patient
j) experienced
k) willing to try new things
l) shares responsibility or empowers others

Give everyone a few minutes to look over their cards and make changes. Ask them to share with a partner the top three qualities they think a leader should have. What made them choose these three?

Variation: Write each of the above qualities on two slips of paper. Shuffle and hand out the slips. Ask group members to find the person who has the same quality as theirs and discuss in pairs: Why is this an important quality for a leader to have? Invite them to summarize this for the rest of the group. Then ask them to place themselves on a continuum from "most important" to "least important," according to how important they think the quality is. Pairs may split up if they disagree.

Youth Concerns

Hand out slips of paper and ask everyone to write down one problem they see in the world or in their local community. Gather the papers and put them in a bowl. Have a group member select a paper and read it aloud. Spend a few minutes brainstorming how youth might take a leadership role in addressing this issue. If group members express feelings of powerlessness around a particular issue, try to discuss why they feel this way. Plan future programs to address concerns expressed.

Youth Leadership

Brainstorm ways that the group might offer leadership in the church or community during Advent. Group members might plan an Advent party to help members of the congregation prepare for Christmas. (See **Youth Participation in Advent and Christmas** on page 67 for some ideas.)

Let's Shake On It!

Write out the list of leadership qualities from the exercise on this page. Ask group members to look at this list and to quietly consider:
• Which of these qualities do you have?
• Which would you like to have?

Ask them to pick one quality they have from the list. Then ask them to get up and shake hands with everyone else, introducing themselves by that quality (e.g. "I'm a good listener") as they exchange handshakes. This is a good "stretcher" and a chance for group members to connect on an individual basis with others.

Types of Leadership

Write the following "roles" on separate squares of paper: Parent, Teacher, Church Minister, Baby Sitter, Sports Coach, Youth Group Leader, Manager, Camp Counselor.

Ask everyone to get into pairs (or small groups). Hand each pair a square. Explain that each square has the name of a different type of leader on it. Ask them to read their square and then write down five qualities they think that leader would have (e.g. the leadership qualities of a church minister will be different from those of a baby sitter).

Ask one pair to read out the five qualities they listed. The rest of the group guesses which leader has those qualities. Continue with the rest of the groups. Talk about the leadership qualities the different groups listed. What qualities would you add to these lists? What does it take to be a good leader?

Traffic Jam

See page 37 for the instructions for this game. This game is best solved when some group members take on a leadership role. Do not suggest this to the group in the beginning – allow them to discover this for themselves.

After the game, talk about how everyone felt playing it. Was it difficult? What helped you solve the puzzle? Do you feel good about your role in it? What did you learn about leadership as a result of this game?

Today's Leaders

Give everyone a few minutes in pairs or small groups to look through magazines and newspapers and circle headlines, articles, or pictures of people who are leaders in the world today. Share the results in the larger group.

Talk about the different leadership styles these examples represent. Imagine that one of these leaders can come to lead your group. Whom would group members invite? Why? Did any of the newspapers or magazines feature any young people as leaders? Do you know of any young people who have been or are leaders in the world today? Who? What difficulties do you think young leaders face? Why do you think a young person would make a good leader?

Mirror, Mirror

Divide the group into pairs. Have them choose which one will be "1" and which will be "2." Lead them through the following exercises:
- To begin, "1" is the leader and "2" is the follower. Invite "1" to initiate a motion and "2" to follow, mirroring the action.
- Then invite "2" to initiate an action and "1" to be the follower.
Have each lead several actions.
- Then have "1" initiate an action and, instead of mirroring the action, invite "2" to add to the action.
- Invite "2" to initiate an action and "1" to add to the action.

When you've finished, talk about the exercise. Which role did you like better, being a leader or follower? Did it get easier as you worked together awhile?

Closing Worship

Related Scripture Passages: Mark 9:33-35, Mark 10:43-45, John 13:13-16
Story: Read the modern parable **King and Queen of All the Land** on page 41.
Prayer or Meditation: Groups can provide leadership opportunities. In advance, ask a member of the group to plan a simple closing. This could be a prayer or a meditation (one they have created or one from a book). Several people can work on this together. Post a sign-up list. If you did the **Youth Concerns** exercise on the previous page, point out that the issues group members identified are possible themes for worship.

Section B: Seasons of Advent & Christmas

Mood and Flavor of these Seasons

The short Seasons of Advent and Christmas are combined in this section, but they are two distinct and different seasons.

The Christian Year begins with the Season of Advent on the Sunday nearest St. Andrew's Day (November 30). Unlike the secular year, which always begins on January 1, the Church Year may begin as early as November 27 or as late as December 3. The season consists of the four weeks leading up to Christmas.

Advent is a season of preparation with a mood of expectation and hope. The word "advent" means "coming." At this time the church focuses on the coming of Christ into the world 2,000 years ago. We also focus on the present possibilities of Christ's rebirth within each of us and in our community. We look to the future and the coming of God's reign of Shalom. As a season of preparation, Advent is also a time when we examine ourselves and confess that our lives and our world are not as God intended. The color for Advent has traditionally been purple, the color of penitence. Recently, to show a difference in mood from Lent, some churches have begun to use the color blue – the color of hope and anticipation. Scripture readings during this season include the prophets' visions of the coming of God's Shalom and of the birth of God's "anointed one" or the Messiah. In the New Testament we read about the coming reign of Christ, in all its fullness, at the end of time.

The Season of Christmas is a joyous one beginning on December 25 (or at sundown on December 24) when we hear about the angels telling the Good News to humble shepherds outside Bethlehem.

Many churches hold candlelight services on Christmas Eve and Christmas Day. The season lasts 12 days, ending with the Feast of Epiphany on January 6. The colors for the season are white and gold (or yellow).

Special Days

Some special days occur during Advent. World AIDS Day is December 1*. International Human Rights Day is December 10, marking the signing of the International Declaration of Human Rights. Although these are not part of the Christian Year, many churches recognize these in some way. During Advent some churches have a "white gift" service to collect gifts for Christmas hampers or food banks.

In addition to the special days of Christmas Eve and Christmas Day, the Season of Christmas includes the Feast of Epiphany on January 6. It is the "twelfth day" of Christmas and marks the end of the Christmas Season. The feast celebrates the visit of the Magi to the home of Jesus. Of course, the secular year begins in this season with the celebrations of New Year's Eve and New Year's Day.

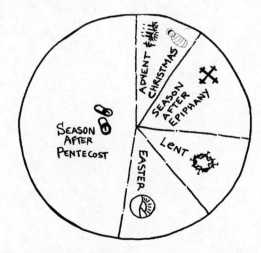

* In some years this date may fall in the Season after Pentecost.

Implications for Youth Ministry

The strong social justice themes of the Season after Pentecost continue in the Season of Advent. As we prepare for Christ's coming we are aware of the things that are not as they should be, and we look at how we can effect change. By Advent most youth group members have developed ties with one another and feelings of trust. They are ready to try new things. They may want to offer leadership beyond the group's own small community.

Most churches have activities they traditionally do during Advent – the "Hanging of the Greens," Advent parties, special services, church school pageants, and outreach projects. These events offer opportunities for youth participation and leadership.

The hard work of group-building throughout the fall yields results when group members work together, combining their talents and interests, to plan a worship service, lead an event, or carry out a project (see **Youth Participation in Advent and Christmas** on page 67). Afterwards take time to learn from the experience. Evaluate together what happened. Did we plan well and follow through on everything? Are there things we would do differently another time? What parts can we affirm and celebrate? Sometimes we forget to evaluate together even though this can be a valuable learning experience for group members. Whether you've completed a project or not, take time as a group to evaluate fall programs. Then plan and dream together about the coming months.

Idea Page #1 Expectation and Hope

Group Check-in

The word "advent" means "coming." What's coming in your lives as Christmas approaches? Ask everyone to turn to the person next to them. Talk for a minute about what they know or expect will happen in the next few weeks (e.g. exams, end of term, visiting relatives, Christmas party at work). Invite everyone to take a turn introducing their partner and telling the rest of the group one of the things that's "coming" in that person's life.

Alarm Bells

Hide several alarm clocks around your meeting space set to go off within five minutes of beginning the game. The aim is to find all the clocks before they ring. Ready,

 set, go!

Ask everyone to share how they felt playing this game. How are these feelings similar to the feelings associated with this time of year? Advent is often a busy time of preparation – shopping, studying for exams, getting ready for out-of-town visitors, attending parties. It's easy to get caught up in the "hustle and bustle" and forget to focus on Christ's coming into the world.

Discuss how group members are preparing this Advent. If we are really going to put Christ at the center of our plans and our lives, how will we prepare differently this year?

Advent Outreach

- Plan to support a community service program. Organize a fund raiser (see **Youth Participation in Advent and Christmas** on page 67).
- Plan to attend or take part in an alternative worship service for people who are feeling less-than-merry as Christmas approaches.
- Plan your own Christmas party. Include time in the agenda for baking, preparing for a fund raiser, or planning involvement in a worship service.

Advent Analogies

Write the following on four different pieces of paper:
- a crowded mall
- a walk in the woods
- a snowflake
- a fire truck

Post the signs in four corners of your meeting space.

Ask everyone to describe how this time of year feels to them by choosing one of the signs to complete this sentence: "To me Advent feels most like..." Have everyone stand by "their" sign. Ask those who chose the same analogy to discuss why they feel that way.

Difficult Seasons

There are many feelings associated with Advent and Christmas. For some people this is the happiest time of the year and for others it is the most stressful and difficult time of year. What people do you think find this season a difficult time? How do others reach out to these people? Take time to talk about the various organizations that reach out to people in need (e.g. parents who can't afford gifts, homeless people, the bereaved, patients in hospitals). What special programs are organized by groups in the community in this season? What special programs are organized by the church?

Advent Wreaths

You will need: Styrofoam wreaths, sharp art knife, two different shades of green construction paper or felt, scissors, white glue, cardboard holly leaf patterns for tracing, five candles for each person – three light purple/dark blue, one pink and one free-standing, large white candle.

Instructions: Trace the base of a taper on the wreath in four places, equal distance from one another. (This will ensure you'll have a perfect fit for the candles.) Using a sharp art knife, cut about 3/4 of the way into the wreath, hollowing out the parts inside the circles. Test with a taper to make sure the holes are deep enough to support the candles. Cut holly leaves from construction paper (or felt) using cardboard leaf patterns. Glue these to the wreath, overlapping them to get the desired effect. (Do not cover the holes you have cut for the candles.) Cut round circles from red construction paper for holly berries. Glue on. Place the white candle in the center of the wreath (symbolizing Jesus).

Use these wreaths as table centerpieces. Light one candle for each of the four weeks of Advent, the pink one on the third Sunday and the white candle on Christmas morning.

Advent Candles

You will need: a white, 8-inch (20cm) taper for each person, fine-line markers, rulers

Instructions: Make a 25-day candle! Give everyone a white taper. Using a ruler, make 25 marks on the wax, evenly spaced, from top to bottom. Leave about 2 in. (5cm) at the bottom so marks are not hidden when the candle is inserted into a holder. Circle the candle with a thin marker line at each of these marks.

It is easy in the busyness of our Christmas preparations – shopping, wrapping, writing exams – to forget the real reason for our celebrations. Encourage group members to use these candles to help remain focused on their Advent preparations. Light the candle each day during Advent and spend some time praying or just sitting quietly to think, letting the candle melt down to the next line on the candle before extinguishing it.

A Ban on Christmas

In pairs or small groups discuss this situation: Christmas has just been declared illegal by the government (as it was in 1644 in England by the Puritan government). What difference will it make? What difference will it make to Christians, not to have a Christmas celebration?

Plan a Christmas celebration for a time when Christmas is banned. What would it be like? How would it be different? the same? For you, what is "essential" to Christmas? What would you miss? What would you not miss? What difference would it make to your family's plans? Have everyone come together and share their ideas.

Closing Worship

Related Scripture Passages: Isaiah 9:2-7, Luke 1:26-56
Story: Read the story **Nothing Is Found That Is Not Looked For** on the next page.
Prayer: Read together **A Litany of Remembering** on page 61.

Nothing Is Found That Is Not Looked For

After the shepherds had been to see the Christ Child in Bethlehem, they made their way back to their sheep telling everyone they met about the wondrous things they had seen. Soon, more and more people were crowding around them to hear the story of the baby born in the stable. While they talked, their flocks grazed around them, seemingly unaware of what was happening.

But two lambs overheard what the shepherds were saying and decided to move closer. When they heard all that the shepherds had related the bigger lamb wondered, "I would like to see this child myself. But how will we find him?"

"Nothing is found that is not looked for," said the smaller lamb. "We look for grass to eat and water to drink. So we can look for the Christ Child. We could go tonight." So they set off on their adventure, skipping and springing down the grassy slopes toward Bethlehem. After a while they came to a shepherd's cottage. "Could this be the stable the shepherds were describing?" the bigger lamb wondered.

"Nothing is found that is not looked for," said the smaller lamb as she butted her head against the door of the cottage. The door creaked

open slightly and the two lambs poked their heads around it. But they didn't see a baby. They didn't find what they were looking for, so they continued on. They went further and further, and now the bigger lamb began to fret, "I wonder where the stable is? We should have found it by now. We were foolish to come so far. We'll get lost. Maybe we are already lost. Do you know how to get back to the fields? What if we don't find the Christ Child?"

"Nothing is found that is not looked for," said the smaller lamb. "I will look for the baby. You go back to the other sheep."

"We should both go back," said the bigger lamb. "The shepherds are probably looking for us by now! Why won't you come with me?"

"I'm going to go a little further. I'll be all right," said the smaller lamb.

The bigger lamb, being afraid, decided to go back the way it had come and find the shepherds. They would come and rescue this foolish lamb! So he left the smaller lamb, who was looking up at the stars.

The lamb gazed up into the night sky for a long time. Her eyes were fixed on a star that seemed to shine brighter than all the others. She remembered what the shepherds had said about seeing a bright star. "I will go to the place where that star is," she said to herself.

She ran over the fields, over rocks, into the town. She ran through the streets, past the houses, past the inns. Her heart was beating very fast and she was tired. She passed by a stable that smelled sweetly of hay. She felt her stomach grumbling. She looked up at the sky again, but the lights from the town made it hard to see. She could no longer see the bright star. "I really am lost," she said to herself. Weary and discouraged she stopped. Her legs trembled with exhaustion like they had on the day she was born. Slowly she turned back, thinking she might find some cool water to drink at the stable she had passed. Then she heard it. So soft she barely heard it. Then she heard it a second time. A baby crying. The cry was no louder than the bleat of a newly born lamb.

At the entrance to the stable the little lamb stood perfectly still, peering in. Then she saw the baby, lying on the sweet-smelling hay in a manger.

"Nothing is found that is not looked for," she said to herself.

A Litany of Remembering

Leader: O God, when the moment was right, you sent your Son Jesus to live among us. Through Jesus we know your love for us and all the world. As we prepare once again to celebrate Christmas help us remember why we are celebrating. When we make our family plans for Christmas...

All: Help us remember whose birth day it is.

Leader: When we feel the pressure to buy and buy and buy...

All: Help us remember whose birth day it is.

Leader: When we think about all the waste generated by our celebrating – the empty pop cans, the discarded wrappings, the toys that break after a day's use –

All: Help us remember whose birth day it is.

Leader: When we are tempted to avoid those who are hungry, sick, lonely, and in prison...

All: Help us remember whose birth day it is.

Leader: Lord, forgive us when we forget who you are and why you have come. Help us remember and celebrate your birth day by giving of ourselves to those you came to serve. Amen.

World AIDS Day

Group Check-in

Ask everyone to position themselves according to their energy level. Think of the ceiling as the high energy mark (i.e. energetic) and the floor as the low energy mark (i.e. no energy). Group members might sit, lie on the floor, or stand on a chair to express how they're feeling. Once everyone is in position, invite them to look around and notice where others have put themselves on the "energymometer." Does anyone want to share why they are in these positions? Be sensitive to each other's meter reading today.

AIDS Guest Speaker

Invite a guest speaker from a local organization or hospital that works with people living with AIDS or who are HIV-positive. Ask them to talk about their work. What services have been developed? What services are still needed? How has the community responded to the AIDS crisis? How has the church responded?

AIDS Home Video Show

Check with your local library or church resource center for a video about AIDS. There are also many available from your local video store such as "And the Band Played On," "The Cure," or "Philadelphia" that might be good discussion starters. View the whole film or just a clip. (See **Videos and Youth Groups** on page 14.)

World AIDS Day Vigil

Check with local organizations about plans for a vigil for World AIDS Day in your neighborhood. Arrange to attend as a group. Discuss ways you can follow up on the experience (e.g. planning a fund raiser, writing prayers to be included in a Sunday service, creating a display).

AIDS Awareness-Raising

• Fund Raiser: Purchase red ribbon and small safety pins from a craft store to create lapel ribbons for World AIDS Day. Offer these to members of the congregation. Ask for donations to support a local organization that works with those infected with the AIDS virus and their families.

• Display: Gather information about the world AIDS crisis or use the information from the **AIDS Memorial Quilt** on page 65 to create an informational display.

• Drama: Create a short drama or pantomime about the issues faced by persons living with AIDS or HIV. This might focus on the issues of fear, misunderstanding, prejudice, isolation, or lack of adequate medical care. Incorporate this into a worship service on the Sunday nearest to World AIDS Day.

AIDS Memorial Quilt

Hand out copies of **AIDS Memorial Quilt** on pages 65–66. Read it together and give group members time to share their feelings about the AIDS disease. What information would they like to share with others? Plan how to do this.

Making an AIDS Memorial Quilt

Make your own AIDS Memorial Quilt (see next page for background information).
You will need: 2-ply quilted paper towels, washable (non-permanent) markers, ball-point pens, fine-tipped marker.

Instructions: Fold a paper towel in four, crease and unfold. Cut squares apart. Draw a simple design in ball-point pen. Outline the design using washable (non-permanent) markers. You do not need to fill designs in as the ink will "run" when you daub with water. Dip a Q-tip in water and apply this sparingly to the design you have drawn on the paper towel. (*Note:* The towel will absorb the water quickly and make colors run. You might need to experiment with several squares before you get this just right.) Lettering in marker doesn't work well with this method. Add lettering with a fine-tipped marker after the towel is dry, or use ball-point pen (before or after). When the towel is dry, outline or touch up any details using a fine-line marker or ball-point pen. Write information about the spread of AIDS and HIV infection, the names of people in your community or others who are infected or who have died. Sew finished squares together with a simple hem-stitch. (*Note:* This quilt can be made with squares of cotton-polyester fabric using tie-dye or fabric paints. You might find a parent or other adult who quilts to sew this all together with red fabric sashing.)

Closing Worship

Scripture Passage: Matthew 25:31-40
Meditation and Prayer: At the end of the film "And the Band Played On" there is some footage of AIDS vigils that have been held around the world. It also includes footage of various well-known people who are infected or who have died of AIDS or have been advocates for AIDS research. The musical accompaniment is Elton John singing the "The Last Song." One group viewed the film and had a discussion. Then for their closing worship everyone was invited to offer silent or spoken prayers and light candles. They ended by watching the final segment of the video.

AIDS Memorial Quilt

The AIDS Memorial Quilt, also known as the NAMES Project, is made of 3 x 6 ft. (1 x 2m) panels that tell about people who have died from AIDS. It began touring North America in 1992, with the hope that it would raise awareness about HIV and AIDS.

Lucille Teasdale, from Montreal and her husband, Piero Corti, of Italy, both medical doctors, have lived and worked in Uganda for 34 years. They began working in a 40-bed dispensary which has now grown to a 450-bed hospital. It treats thousands of patients each year and trains hundreds of Ugandan doctors and nurses. Their dedication to helping others has earned them the title of "heroes" in the town of Gulu, where they live and work. Being doctors in a country in which 1.5 million are infected with HIV poses risks for these two doctors. In fact, of the approximately 10,000 patients who visit the hospital each year, 40% of those are HIV positive. Despite the risks, Lucille Teasdale has performed more than 13,000 operations. She has cut herself on many occasions, and Lucille has now contracted the AIDS virus. Her husband, Piero, suffers from a heart problem, a sign that the hard work has taken its toll. The couple have calmly accepted their situation, acknowledging that their work in Uganda has blessed them with a richness of experience they could not have had otherwise.

AN AVERAGE OF 6,000 PEOPLE WORLDWIDE ARE BEING INFECTED WITH HIV, THE VIRUS THAT CAUSES AIDS, EVERY DAY. – "AIDS IN THE WORLD," INTERAGENCY COALITION ON AIDS & DEVELOPMENT (ICAD), 1995

Ryan White was born with severe hemophilia – a hereditary disease which prevents blood from clotting properly. Ryan became infected with the AIDS virus from receiving injections of a blood product that is given to hemophiliacs to help their blood clot normally – Factor VIII. The injected blood was contaminated. After recovering from a bout of pneumocystic pneumonia – a rare form of pneumonia that most often strikes people who have AIDS – Ryan tried to return to school, but was told he was not allowed back because people feared he would infect others. Ryan recognized that people were afraid because they didn't understand what AIDS was or how you caught it. He began to speak out on behalf of people suffering from the disease. He was eventually invited to testify before the President's Commission on AIDS. Ryan died on April 8, 1990 at the age of 17.

AIDS Memorial Quilt *(continued)*

It is estimated that Sub-Saharan Africa accounts for more than 60% of the total number of people infected with HIV worldwide. More than 12 million adults and 1 million children have become infected since the onset of the pandemic. – "AIDS in the World," ICAD, 1995

SEVENTY PERCENT OF ALL NEW INFECTIONS IN WOMEN ARE AMONG THOSE 15 TO 24 YEARS OLD. – "WOMEN & HIV/AIDS," ICAD, 1995

In May 1992 Jon Gates gave a speech to the Canadian AIDS Society. In it he called on the government to delay the release of any new vaccines or cures for AIDS. A strange thing for someone infected with AIDS to do. Strange, and courageous. Jon Gates was asking for this not because he did not wish a cure or vaccine for AIDS be found, but because he was concerned that it would only be made available to people who could afford it. "If history is any guide to go by," he said, "our society – once we've discovered those vaccines or cures – will move very quickly to secure the safety of our own populations. Once that has been accomplished, we will promptly forget about the issue, and in the process abandon three-quarters of the world's population to meet their fate as best they can." Gates called for a delay in production until a time when the drug or vaccine could be made affordable worldwide, and until it was accessible and available worldwide. Gates urged those who were infected and affected by the disease to stand in "solidarity" with their brothers and sisters in less-developed countries. Jon Gates died on December 9, 1992, just six months after making this speech.

In the early 1980s, journalist Randy Shilts was the first to provide extensive coverage of the AIDS epidemic that was sweeping San Francisco. At that time, little was known about the disease. It was referred to as "the gay plague" because the majority of people known to be infected were homosexual males. Writing for the *San Francisco Chronicle,* Shilts provided educational information, campaigned for safer sex and demanded the closing of gay bathhouses. Shilts considered the bathhouses a problem because men engaged in sex with many partners there. Shilts criticized his government's cynical indifference toward AIDS victims. By the time President Ronald Reagan delivered his first speech about the epidemic, 20,849 people had already died of the disease. Shilts' tireless efforts were at first ignored or met with hostility. He was booed and spat upon on the streets of his own neighborhood. Shilts felt compelled to continue in spite of this harsh treatment because he was gay himself and "people I cared about and loved" were dying. Shilts tested positive for the HIV virus in 1987, the same day he turned in his manuscript for his monumental history of AIDS, *And the Band Played On,* which has since been made into a well-known movie. Shilts, who died of pneumonia at age 42, was one of an estimated 50,000 Americans who died of AIDS-related illnesses in 1993.

Youth Participation in Advent and Christmas

In preparation for the Seasons of Advent and Christmas, meet with the clergy and leaders in your church to discuss possibilities for youth involvement in the upcoming events. Share the particular interests of group members. Here are some ideas for youth group activities and leadership:

Poinsettias and Visitations

Make a list of sick and shut-in members of the congregation. Check that they would enjoy receiving a poinsettia (and perhaps a short visit). Buy poinsettias from a nursery at a volume discount price. Then invite members of the congregation to buy a poinsettia from the group. Provide buyers with the name and address of an ill or shut-in member of the congregation so they can deliver the plant themselves, perhaps staying for a short visit. (Or have members of the congregation donate the cost of poinsettias and have the group deliver these. Visits could include carol singing!) Choose the delivery date in advance and inform the recipients.

Advent Party

Some youth groups welcome the chance to organize an Advent Party. The party activities and fellowship help families in the congregation prepare for a meaningful Christmas. Make Advent wreaths or crèche scenes for home. Plan an event around a theme like "angels." Offer a variety of craft options suitable for different ages and levels of skill. Plan a short closing worship service on an Advent theme. Organize the "Hanging of the Greens" or setting up the Christmas tree. Or plan a New Year's Eve family party.

"O Little Town of Bethlehem"
Child Care Service

Use the talents of group members to run a drop-in child care service on a Saturday during Advent. Plan to dramatize the story of **The Real St. Nick** (see page 76) do crafts, tell stories, bake, and decorate cookies with the children! Invite parents to drop their kids off for an hour or two or for the whole day. They can use the time to prepare for Christmas (doing their shopping, baking or just having time to themselves). Offer the service free of charge or ask for donations of new toys for an organization like "Santas Anonymous."

Alternative Christmas Service
"Blue Christmas"
or "The Longest Night" Service

Some churches have an alternative Christmas service for people who have recently experienced a loss (death, unemployment, illness) and are feeling less-than-merry. Plan to attend as a group and serve the tea and coffee after the service. Possibly the group could provide some baking that they make together ahead of time. Usually only a handful of people attends these services. The presence of young people can be very touching to those who attend. It's an experience that youth remember long afterwards.

Special Services

Many churches have one or more special services on Christmas Eve. Often these include lots of music and candlelight. Youth might form a small choir, perform a drama or pantomime, or decorate the entrance to the church with candles.

Outreach

Take part in a worship service at a retirement or nursing home, or plan a special visit. Prepare refreshments ahead of time, make a small gift for each person, or make tray decorations for use in a special residents' dinner. Plan to lead the seniors in singing some of their favorite carols.

Idea Page #3

Angels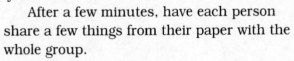

Group Check-in

Explain the classical division of angels into three divisions: archangels (chief angels), seraphim ("fiery ones"), and cherubim (unnatural composite creatures). Ask everyone to choose which one they feel most like, based on the way they are feeling right now. They might have to use their imaginations a bit for this one!

Angel Associations

Cut simple angel shapes from paper for everyone. Hand them out and provide markers. Invite everyone to take a few minutes to express on this paper the thoughts, associations, or images that come to mind when they hear the word "angel." These might be movie titles, physical descriptions, or song lyrics.

After a few minutes, have each person share a few things from their paper with the whole group.

All about Angels

What do you know about angels? Where do we get our ideas about angels? (e.g. the media, the Bible, songs) Look at some pictures of angels from art books, magazines, and greeting cards. Check your local and church library to get a broad sampling – contemporary, medieval, Renaissance.

Divide into small groups with each looking at some of the books and pictures. Ask the groups to think about the following questions:
• What do you know about angels?
• What similarities and differences do you see between the various representations?
• What might these tell you about what people believe about angels?
• What are the angels doing in these pictures?
• Which angels appeal to you the most?
• What do you believe about angels?

The Popularity of Angels

Many people today are interested in angels. Angels appear in the lyrics of popular songs and in movies; they appear on greeting cards. You can buy a "guardian angel" to pin to your sweater. You can even subscribe to an angel newsletter! Ask everyone to share their feelings about the popularity of angels. Why do you think people are interested in angels? What do you think angels signify for others? Some people have strong feelings about the way angels have become a consumer "fad." Some think our society has taken something sacred and made it into a "golden calf." Others think it is a positive, non-threatening way for non-religious people to be exposed to an aspect of God.

Ask group members what they think about angels. What do angels signify for them? Do they believe in angels?

Angels Home Video Show

Take advantage of the current popularity of angels in our media and watch a video about angels together. (See **Youth and Videos** on page 14.) Talk afterwards about how the angels in the film were depicted. What functions did they seem to have? How does this relate to the function of angels as they appear in the Bible? (See **The Four Functions of Angels** on the next page.)

Stories about Angels

What stories about angels do you know from the Bible? How many stories do you think there are in the Bible about angels (many, not many, a few)? There are more than 75 references to angels in the Bible!

Together look at some of these stories. Divide into groups of three or four and have each look up a different passage. Ask them to present this story to the other groups (e.g. dramatically, miming while a narrator reads, retelling in their own words).

After each presentation, try to identify which function the angel in that story was performing (see **The Four Functions of Angels** on this page). Suggested passages:

Gen. 28:10-17   Num. 22:22-35
Judges 13:2-23   Acts 12:6-17
Rev. 12:7-12   Matt. 4:1-11
Matt. 28:1-7

Angel T-Shirts

Invite everyone to sketch a design or slogan onto a T-shirt (or pillowcase) with fabric crayons or paints. Remember that one of the functions of angels is to be "message bearers." Likewise, T-shirts can bear a message to others. Ask everyone to think carefully about the slogan or image they choose to put on their shirt.

**The Four Functions
of Angels**

Angels...

bear messages from God to
God's people

act as instruments of
God's justice

protect the people

praise God

Hymns about Angels

Look at your church hymnary for hymns that mention angels. (Many of these you'll find in the section of hymns traditionally sung at Christmas.) Sing or read these together. Talk about the images of angels in these hymns. What might this suggest about what the person who wrote the song believed about angels? How does this fit with your beliefs about angels? Try to identify which function the angel is performing (see **The Four Functions of Angels** above).

Closing Worship

Related Scripture Passages: Luke 1:26-38, Luke 2:8-20
Meditation: *(Light incense or a scented candle.)*

• Ask someone to bring Angel Cards™. Place them face down in the center of the circle. Invite everyone, one at a time, to select a card. Allow a few minutes of silence (or play some quiet music). Invite them to think about the word they chose and how it might relate to their lives right now. Encourage them to remember that word and to think about what significance it might have for them as they go about their lives in the coming week.

• Alternatively, write phrases on slips of paper that were said by or about angels like "Nothing will be impossible for God" (the Angel Gabriel in Lk. 1:37) or "Worship God who made heaven, earth, sea, and the springs of water!" (the angel of the Lord in Rev. 14:7c). Invite everyone to choose one phrase and to reflect on the significance of it for their lives.

Idea Page #4 Violence and the Media

Group Check-in

Invite group members to check in by naming their favorite TV programs. Record these on newsprint. (Use these if you do **TV Continuum** below.) Which ones do they try never to miss? Why?

TV Continuum

1. Have everyone list their favorite TV programs on a sheet of newsprint.
2. Imagine a line running from one end of the room to the other. Label one end of the room "Just like me" and the other end "Not like me at all."
3. Choose one of the TV programs. Ask youth to consider how the lifestyle depicted in the program compares with their own.
4. Have everyone place themselves on the line between "just like me" and "not like me at all."
5. Then, using the same process, ask the youth to consider how the relationships depicted and the values promoted in the program compare with their own.

Afterwards, gather together and discuss these questions:
- What do you like about this TV show?
- Would you like to live in a world like the one shown in this program?
- Is the show interesting to you because it is so much like "real life" or because it is so different from your own experience?
- What kind of values do you think this program promotes? (e.g. importance of family, individualism, violence as an acceptable response to conflict, concern for others)
- How do you think God would rate this program – do you think it reflects the kind of relationships, self-image, values and lifestyles God intended for us?

5. Complete continuums for other programs in the same way.
6. Share thoughts about how the media influence what our society considers healthy or unhealthy, normal or average, good or bad.

Alien Viewpoints

Ask everyone to imagine they are aliens from another planet. Because of a shortage of food and water on their own planet, they have been sent to observe earthlings, gather information on the earthlings' society, and make a decision whether or not earthlings would be friendly toward them and willing to share their planet with an alien race. Is earthling society peaceful or warlike? Are earthlings selfish or willing to share?

Unfortunately the aliens do not all reach the same conclusion. (Divide the "aliens" into two groups.) The first group comes to the decision that humans are a violent race – greedy and warlike. The second group believes humans are essentially a peace-loving and generous people. Both groups have to report their findings to their leader, Emperor Neila. Provide each group with newspapers and news magazines to search for "evidence" to support their claims (e.g. pictures, advertisements, news articles). When they are ready, have them present their reports. Then discuss these questions:
- How accurately do the media portray our society?
- Was it easier to find examples of "good" or "bad" aspects of our society?
- Do you think the media focus on the negative aspects of our society? Or do they just "tell it like it is"?
- Do you think the media influence the way we see ourselves as a society?

Violence in the Media

Borrow materials on violence in the media from your local library or church resource center. Use these as discussion starters to talk about the effect of violence in the media on our culture.

Competition or Cooperation?

Have the traditional Tug of War and then try the **Tug of Peace** (see page 34). Talk about the differences. How did your body feel when you prepared to do the Tug of War? the Tug of Peace? What different feelings do you associate with competition and cooperation? How do you think the competition in our games and sports affects our culture? How does society encourage competition? How does it encourage cooperation?

Think of another competitive game (e.g. musical chairs). How can you change the rules to make it cooperative?

Fishbowl

Gather in a circle. Ask four volunteers to sit on cushions in the center. Read aloud **The Sunday Times** article below. Then ask the four people to begin the discussion, remembering that they are representing the viewpoints of the creators of this so-called "C-Chip."

Those on the outside of the circle can only listen, not comment. If someone wants to join the discussion they may tap the shoulder of someone in the circle and take their place. They shouldn't tap the shoulder of someone who hasn't had a chance to speak. Encourage those on the outside to give those in the middle a few minutes to discuss before replacing someone.

When the discussion appears to be at a lull or conclusion, ask the four to join the circle and reflect together as a group.

- Why do you think Christians would or should care about these things?
- Have you ever chosen not to watch a program, or a certain type of program, because you thought it promoted inappropriate behavior, exploited people, or reinforced stereotypes? (e.g. about men, women, teenagers)
- What difference do you think one person can make by choosing either to watch or not to watch a particular show?

THE SUNDAY TIMES

A recent breakthrough in technology has Christian television viewers praising its creators! The Christian Chip, or C-Chip, filters out unwanted messages, including advertisements, that Christians feel do not "fit" with their beliefs and value system – that modeled on the example of Jesus Christ. Programs that show a high level of hypocrisy, greed, apathy and injustice are screened out by an electronic chip, no larger than a Eucharistic wafer. While there are still a few bugs to work out, (insert the name of one of the four volunteers), a spokesperson for the group that invented the chip, says the group is working hard to make the chip available as soon as possible. "It's a matter of deciding what's acceptable to a Christian viewer," (he/she) said. The group of inventors met recently at (insert the name of your church), the headquarters of the group. They deliberated over a list of popular programs, weeding out those that exceed acceptable levels of injustice and hypocrisy. Rumor has it that the list includes such Neilson-rating favorites as (choose three or four programs – include a sitcom, a nature show, a talk show, a cartoon or news program).

© Cheryl Perry, 1996. Used by permission.

Closing Worship

Related Scripture Passages: Psalm 55:4-11, Isaiah 11:2-9, Matthew 26:47-54

Prayer: O God, help us to live our lives honestly,
to be true to what we say we believe,
and to make room for new understandings. Amen.

Idea Page #5 # Seasonal Celebrations

Group Check-in

In advance, ask everyone to bring an ornament from home that they would normally hang on their Christmas tree. (Alternatively, ask everyone to draw a symbol of Advent or Christmas.) What ornament (symbol) has the most meaning for you? Take turns sharing the memories that made it meaningful for you. See the box below to talk about the original meaning of some of the symbols of these seasons.

An Advent Prayer Tree

Place a fir bough in a bucket of sand or plaster of Paris. Cut simple Advent symbols out of white paper (e.g. bell, angel, candy cane). Hole punch these and tie lengths of silver or gold string or yarn through these so they can be hung on the tree. As people arrive at your gathering, have them write their family name and first names of family members on a paper shape and hang this on the tree. As part of your closing worship, have each one take a paper shape (not their own) off the tree. Ask them to hang the paper ornament on their Christmas tree at home and encourage them to remember that family or persons in their mealtime or family prayers during Advent.

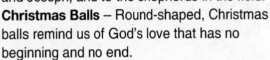

Advent and Christmas Symbols

Bells – For centuries bells hung high in church steeples announced special occasions and good news. Christmas bells symbolize the good news of Jesus' birth.

Angel – The word angel means "messenger." Like the bell, an angel communicates good news to people. Angels appeared to both Mary and Joseph, and to the shepherds in the field.

Christmas Balls – Round-shaped, Christmas balls remind us of God's love that has no beginning and no end.

Christmas Tree – The tree is an evergreen, symbol of everlasting life – the good news that Jesus' death and resurrection proclaimed to all humanity.

Stocking – Some of the coins that St. Nicholas tossed landed in stockings hung to dry by the fireplace.

Star – The star helped the Magi find the Christ Child. Jesus is also called the "bright morning star" in the Book of Revelation.

Gifts – Our gifts can remind us of the gifts the Magi presented to the young Jesus. Mincemeat reminds us of the spices given by the Magi.

Lights and Candles – The book of Isaiah and John talk about the Messiah as one coming to be light in the darkness.

Candy Canes – A candy cane reminds us of the staff the shepherds used. In the Gospel of Luke, the shepherds were the first people to hear the good news of Jesus' birth.

New Year Evaluations and Planning

Evaluate the year and do some planning for the coming months. Use an evaluation tool like **Group Time Line** on page 101 or **Community Links** on page 34.

Advent Event

Use the following suggestions to plan a group or intergenerational event. (See also **Youth Participation in Advent and Christmas** on page 67.)

1. Choosing the Theme

One youth group planned a party for the afternoon of Reign of Christ Sunday, the last Sunday in the Christian Year. They chose a "New (Church) Year's Eve" theme. At their potluck dinner, the table was set with store-bought Christmas crackers and New Year's horns. Everyone broke open their crackers, put on their hats and had an old fashioned countdown to usher in the new Church Year. Everyone was invited to pass the peace in place of the usual hugging and "Happy New Year's" to reflect the focus on the beginning of the Season of Advent and a new Church Year.

Use some of the ideas on pages 69-70 to plan a party around the theme of angels. Or focus on preparing and making Advent wreaths (see page 58). This will encourage families to continue preparing for Advent in their own homes.

2. Food

Plan a potluck meal to follow (or precede) the event. If this is a congregational event, pick a time that will be suitable for both families with small children and seniors.

3. Using Candle Light

Create a worshipful atmosphere by decorating the entrance to the church with **Tin Can Luminaries** (see page 77).

4. Planning Worship

The Season of Advent is a time to prepare for Christmas. Help people focus on the real cause for celebration – the birth of Christ – by focusing your worship on the things we need to let go of in order to experience Christmas this year. How do our preparations reflect what is important to us? The youth might perform a playlet like *Prepare!* by Ralph Middlecamp
(Modern Liturgy, 160 East Virginia St., #290, San Jose, CA 95112).

5. Crafts

Approach "crafty" people in the congregation who might be willing to help out (e.g. someone who silk-screens cards or recycles old cards, makes wooden mangers or tree ornaments). If you are planning an event for all ages, remember to provide several craft options that require different levels of skill and encourage different age groups to work together.

6. Storytelling

Tell (or dramatize) the story **The Real St. Nick** on page 76 for small children. Give them chocolate coins when you are finished or hide coins around the room or sanctuary. Let the children enjoy finding them, the way the poor man's daughters discovered the coins tossed through the window.

7. Inviting a Special Guest

Invite someone who has visited the Holy Land to participate in worship. Ask them to speak (and show slides) to give people a sense of what that first Christmas was like.

Closing Worship

Related Scripture Passages: Luke 3:3-6, Mark 1:1-8
Prayer: Read the **Candle Lighting Litany** on the next page. If you made an **Advent Prayer Tree** (see previous page), encourage participants to remove a symbol with a family's name printed on it (not their own), and take it home with them. Encourage them to remember that family in their prayers throughout Advent and Christmas.

Candle Lighting Litany

(Set up a large central candle and hand out candles to all participants.)

Leader: This candle is a symbol of Jesus, "the light of the world," who came to reflect God's light, God's ways, clearly to each of us. *(Leader lights Christ candle.)* We, too, are called to be light in our world. *(Invite group members to come forward, one at a time and light their candle from the central Christ candle and join in a litany prayer.)* O God, in our world where there is darkness,

ALL: Let us be light.

Leader: When we see others who are hurt, lonely or afraid,

ALL: Let us be light.

Leader: When someone is being left out or treated unfairly,

ALL: Let us be light.

Leader: Whenever and wherever we see things in our world that are not as you intended,

ALL: Let us be light.

Leader: Help us to truly be your disciples in the world.

ALL: Amen.

The Real St. Nick

Saint Nicholas was born long, long ago in a small town in what is now Turkey. Nicholas decided to become a priest and later he became a bishop. He was put in prison for being a Christian. Nicholas was a kind and generous man and many stories were told about him. This is one of the most famous.

A long time ago, in the fourth century AD, there lived a Bishop named Nicholas. Nicholas lived in a small town in Turkey. In that town there also lived a man who lived alone with his three daughters. The oldest daughter was ready to be married. But this man was so poor that he had no money for the marriage. In those days the father had to give a bag of money to the husband-to-be when his daughter got married. Without it a wedding could not happen. Now the man and his daughters were very sad. Nicholas heard of their trouble. In the middle of the night, he went to the house where the man and his daughters lived. He tossed gold coins through an open window near the fireplace. In the morning, the family discovered the gold coins on the floor – some had landed in the stockings hung by the fire to dry. You can imagine their excitement! Now the eldest daughter could be married. What a celebration!

Then time came for the next daughter to marry. Again, in the middle of the night, Nicholas threw gold coins through the open window. By now the family was getting very curious about who the kind and generous person was.

When it came time for the third daughter to marry, the father stayed up all night to try to find out who was helping them. Just as Nicholas was about to throw the gold through the window, the father caught him. The man was surprised to find that it was the bishop. Nicholas asked the man not to tell anyone, but of course it was hard for the man to keep Nicholas' kindness a secret – and that's why we have the story to this very day.

St. Nicholas is known by many different names around the world. In France he is called Père Noel. In England he is called Father Christmas. In Holland he is called Sinterklaas. Do you know what we call St. Nicholas here? Each year at Christmas we remember the kindness and generosity that St. Nicholas showed people as a follower of Jesus – we remember him through the stories we tell of Santa Claus.

Stars

Group Check-in

Ask everyone to compare themselves to a planet in the solar system or some other galactic phenomenon like a nova, comet, or moon dust. Take turns describing the "space" you are in to each other.

Stargazing

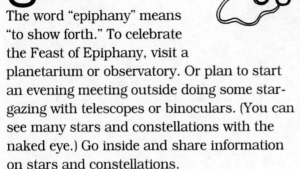

The word "epiphany" means "to show forth." To celebrate the Feast of Epiphany, visit a planetarium or observatory. Or plan to start an evening meeting outside doing some stargazing with telescopes or binoculars. (You can see many stars and constellations with the naked eye.) Go inside and share information on stars and constellations.

Star Qualities

Cut stars from yellow construction paper. Give everyone a star asking them to write their name in its center. Then ask them to pass their star to the person on their left (so that everyone has someone else's star). Invite group members to write one "star" quality they think that person has on a ray of the star. Then pass the stars to the next person. When the stars return to their owners, give everyone an opportunity to read aloud the qualities written on their star.

Tin Can Luminaries

You will need: large and small nails, 10 (284mL) or 14 oz. (397mL) can* for each person, hammers, towels, votive candles

Instructions: Draw a symbol of a star on a piece of paper. Tape it securely to the side of the can. Place the can on its side on a folded towel. Using hammers and nails, carefully punch holes along the outline of the design. Remove the paper pattern when finished and melt ice with hot water. Dry the can and place a small candle in the bottom.

*Remove the label and top of the can. Fill with water and freeze (leave some room for expansion when the water freezes).

Avenue of the Stars

Make an avenue of the stars a la Hollywood Boulevard! On a long strip of newsprint, invite group members to cut and paste a yellow star with their name on it. Below their star make colorful hand prints after placing their hands palm-down in a contrasting color of tempera paint. Be sure to take pictures of the "celebrities" as they are added to the avenue of the stars.

Hand out paper and pens and invite everyone to become "reporters." Get into pairs to interview each other. Then write short biographies on one another to mount near their stars. Use questions from **Roving Reporter** on page 80 or design your own. Add pictures once they're developed. Display this Avenue of the Stars in a prominent place. Members of the congregation can read it and learn more about the youth in their church family.

Society Stars

Who are some of the "stars" in our society? What qualities do these people have that qualify them as stars in society's eyes? Which of these qualities do you think are important to God? What qualities do you have?

If you did the **Star Qualities** activity on this page, ask everyone to read again the "star" qualities identified for them. Did any of these qualities surprise you? (i.e. qualities you haven't considered yourself to have) Which qualities do you think are most important to God?

The Star as a Symbol

Astronomers and astrologists have carefully researched the Christmas Star. Hand out copies of **"We have seen his star"** on the next page. Give everyone time to read it and then ask them to share their reactions.

Discuss:
- The different opinions in the article.
- The different opinions and beliefs of group members about the Christmas Star.
- The star as a symbol. It is an Epiphany symbol. What do stars symbolize to you?

Closing Worship

Related Scripture Passages: Psalm 8, Numbers 24:17, Matthew 2:1-12, Revelation 22:16.

Prayer: Place glow-in-the-dark stars on the ceiling or wall. When the room is darkened these give the surprise effect of a star-filled night sky. (These can be purchased in most craft stores and are adhesive-backed. If you cannot put these on the walls or ceiling of your meeting space, consider sticking them to pieces of paper and taping them on.) Use **Tin Can Luminaries**, if you did this activity, or ordinary candles. Sit in a circle. Each member of the group places their unlit tin can luminary or candle in front of them. Place a large white candle in the center of the circle. Darken the room.

> O God, you revealed yourself to us in the form of a tiny baby
> Who became a child, a teenager, a young adult.
> That single life brought such light into the world.

(Light the large, central candle. Pass the matches around so that one by one the group members light their luminaries. If using candles, one youth can light their candle from the large one; then using their own candle, they light the candle of the one next to them. Continue "passing" the light around the circle until all the candles are lit.)

> Help us spread your light to the darkest corners of our world,
> To the people hidden in shadows who need to know your love.
> Illumine us, O God, that we might help reveal your presence in the world.
> Amen.

The Christmas Star

"We have seen his star"

The five-pointed star, or Christmas Star, is unique. It represents the star said to have appeared above Bethlehem at the time of Jesus' birth. Some astrologers from the East saw the star and took it as a sign of an important event. They set out following it. According to Matthew's Gospel, when the wise men arrived at Herod's palace in Jerusalem they asked the king, "Where is the baby born to be the king of the Jews? We saw his star when it came up in the east, and we have come to worship him."

Astronomers today say they know of no new star that would have appeared any time near the probable date of Jesus' birth. Aside from novas (new stars which appear from time to time), the same stars that appear in our sky today appeared in the skies nearly two thousand years ago. What was this special Christmas star that the wise ones were said to have followed? Some have suggested that the star may have been a meteor, or "shooting star." Astrologers argue with this theory. They point out that meteors appear in the sky for just a few brief seconds as they pass through the Earth's atmosphere. According to the biblical account, the wise men followed the star for many months. Modern astrologers also insist that the star could not have been a comet, though these can be seen with the naked eye for days or even months. Astrologers today know what comets were close to Earth hundreds and thousands of years ago; they say no such comet passed through Earth's atmosphere near the time of Jesus' birth.

Many astronomers and historians today believe that Jesus was not born in 1 AD, but rather in the spring of the year 6 BC. At that time the planets of Mars, Jupiter and Saturn were close together in the sky, forming a triangle in the group of stars known as Pisces. Some astrologers today believe that the wise men, who were also astrologers and studied the movement of the stars and planets, may have taken this as a sign of a significant event. (They knew, for example, that according to Jewish rabbis Mars, Jupiter and Saturn had appeared together in Pisces a few years before the birth of Moses. The constellation of Pisces, therefore, was considered to be the special constellation of the Jewish people. The Wise Men may have seen the grouping of these planets as a sign that a great event had happened in Jewish history.)

Today many people still believe that on the night Jesus was born the special star did appear, a miraculous sign in the sky above Bethlehem.

The star of David is also a symbol for Jesus who was a descendant of King David. Stars (the star of David or the six-pointed star) are also considered symbols for Jesus who was described as "the bright morning star."

Roving Reporter

Interview Sheet

Instructions: You have only a few minutes to interview each other. You may not have time to ask all the questions. Choose a few that interest you the most. When the group comes together again be prepared to share what you found out about your partner.

1. What is your full name? Are you named after anyone? Do you have a nickname?

   _____

2. What is your birth date? Do you know of anyone else who is also born the same month and day as you (e.g. someone famous)?

   _____

3. What was the highlight of your summer?

   _____

4. What do you like to do on Saturday afternoons?

   _____

5. If you could have a guest for dinner from anywhere in the world, who would you invite?

   _____

6. What's your pet peeve (i.e. something that really bugs you)?

   _____

7. What would you do if you had a million dollars?

   _____

8. Name a positive quality you possess.

   _____

Idea Page #7

Gifts and Talents

Group Check-in

Here's a fun way to find out what everyone did over the holidays! Wrap a gift (e.g. a snack) in layers of newsprint for the whole group to share. On each layer write a description of whom the gift should be given to (e.g. "To: Someone who went to church with their family on Christmas day" or "To: Someone who watched more than two movies over the holidays"). As each layer is unwrapped, have the person doing the unwrapping read out the description. Group members who fit the description should identify themselves. The person unwrapping passes the gift to one of these people who then unwraps the next layer, and so on. Try to arrange that each member of the group has a turn unwrapping a layer. The final layer should be addressed to the whole group.

A Gift from God

Have you ever thought of yourself as a gift – a gift from God to the world? Read aloud the poem **Persons Are Gifts** on this page by someone who imagined people as gifts.

What are some of the kinds of gifts mentioned? (e.g. beautiful, ordinary, loosely wrapped, tightly wrapped) Ask everyone to get into pairs and discuss this question with their partner: If you had to describe yourself as a wrapped gift, which gift would you choose and why?

Gift Wrap

Gather in a circle and hand out a sheet of newsprint and marker to each group member. Ask them to write their name in the center.

Explain that this is their piece of gift wrapping paper. Ask them to pass their piece of gift wrap to the person next to them so that everyone has another group member's piece of paper in front of them. Encourage them to write affirmations about a gift or talent they think that group member has. Use the phrase "Thanks for sharing your gift of...with the group." Continue to pass these sheets around the circle so that each member of the group has a chance to write an affirmation about each of the other members. When these return to their owners, everyone reads what others have written about them. Ask them to share their reactions to the words on their paper.

Persons Are Gifts

Persons are gifts which God sent to me...wrapped!
Some are wrapped very beautifully; they are very attractive when I first see them.
Some come in very ordinary wrapping paper.
Others come "special delivery."
Some persons are gifts which come very loosely wrapped; others very tightly.

The wrapping is not the gift!
It is so easy to make this mistake...
It's amusing when babies do it.
Sometimes the gift is very easy to open up.
Sometimes I need others to help.
Is it because they are afraid? Does it hurt?
Maybe they have been opened up before and thrown away! Could it be that the gift is not for me?

I am a person. Therefore, I am a gift too!
A gift to myself, first of all. God gave myself to me.
Have I really looked inside the wrappings? Afraid to?
Perhaps I've never accepted the gift that I am...
Could it be that there is something else inside the wrapping than what I think there is?
Maybe I've never seen the wonderful gift that I am.
Could God's gifts be anything but beautiful?
I love the gift which those who love me give to me; why not this gift from God?

And I am a gift to other persons.
Am I willing to be given by God to others?...
A person for others!
Do others have to be content with the wrappings... never permitted to enjoy the gift?

Every meeting of persons is an exchange of gifts.
Friendship is a relationship between persons who see themselves as they truly are: Gifts of God to each other, for others.
Persons are gifts, gifts received and gifts given.

Adapted from "Friendship Is Eucharist"
by Fr. G.E.Nintemann, O.P.

Talents in Service

Plan to do a service project that combines the gifts and talents of group members. See **Service Project Ideas** in Section F.

Gifts and Talents Show

Host a talent show for your church or have one just with group members. Contact youth ahead of time so they will have an opportunity to prepare their "act" (individually or several of the group members together). See the Category Suggestions below. Award prizes to each participant or a ribbon using **The "Very Gifted" Award** pattern on this page.

Award Category Suggestions
- Most environmentally friendly act
- Most dramatic act
- Most humorous act
- Most graceful act
- Briefest act (for the act that took the least amount of time)
- Loudest act

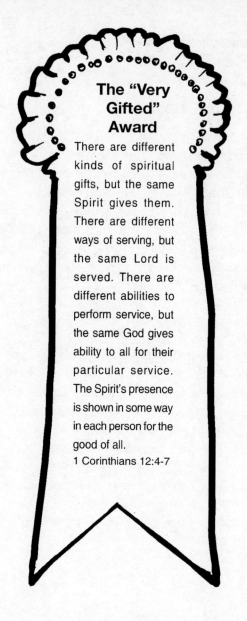

The "Very Gifted" Award

There are different kinds of spiritual gifts, but the same Spirit gives them. There are different ways of serving, but the same Lord is served. There are different abilities to perform service, but the same God gives ability to all for their particular service. The Spirit's presence is shown in some way in each person for the good of all.
1 Corinthians 12:4-7

Closing Worship

Related Scripture Passage: 1 Corinthians 12:4-11
Meditation: Read **The Fourth Wise Man** on the next page. Then do this guided meditation.

Guided Meditation – What Gifts Do I Have to Offer?

(Invite everyone to get into a comfortable position, close their eyes, and concentrate on their breathing for a few minutes. As you read the meditation, pause after each sentence to give everyone time to reflect on what you are saying.)

Imagine you are in another place. It is a dark night and you are outside, looking up at the night sky filled with stars. Take a deep breath. What are you feeling? You look up and see a star in the sky, brighter than all the other stars. You are walking, watching the star, following it. You have been walking for a long time. Concentrate on what the ground beneath your feet feels like. You are coming slowly towards a city. Look around you. What do you see? What sounds do you hear? You continue walking into the city. You see a house. You walk towards it. You come to the door. It is open. You step inside. You see Mary and Joseph and the child, Jesus. You have been traveling for a long time, searching for this place. Finally, you have found it. How do you feel? You step towards the child and look down at your hands. There is the gift you have brought. A symbol of yourself. Something special you have been waiting to give him. What do you do next?

(After a few minutes, invite the youth to slowly come back to the present. Invite them to sit up when they are ready and rejoin the group.)

The Fourth Wise Man

Most people think that there were only three wise men, but I know differently. I was the fourth. Oh, I wasn't really a wise man – just an apprentice. I used to clean the shop, feed the camels, put the books back in the library. I had only just turned twelve at the time.

We were all very excited when Balthazar saw a new star rising at dawn one morning. My masters knew right away that it was the sign they had been waiting for, a star which told of the birth of a baby born to be King of the Jews. Quickly preparations were made for the journey to Palestine. All was excitement and bustle. But, at the last moment, I was left behind. I was too young, they said, the way was long and hard, and besides, someone had to stay home and mind the shop.

I was most upset. I felt that something very special was happening, something in which I just had to participate. Three days later I could stand it no longer. All I had was my little donkey – my masters had taken the camels – and I had no expensive gift to take, only three silver coins. But I closed up shop and set off for Jerusalem. I, too, wanted to find the baby born to be King of the Jews.

The way was not easy. Often I was hungry and thirsty and very tired. But still I kept on. One day, as I was passing a small hut set in the lee of some hills, I heard some weeping. Tying my donkey to a bush, I stooped through the low doorway and entered. Inside was an old woman, crying. "My son is dead," she sobbed. "All I have left is a small herd of goats. Without my son to tend them, the goats will run away, and then I shall starve and die myself."

What could I do? I wanted so much to get to Jerusalem, but I couldn't leave her to die! "Don't worry, Grandmother," I said. "I will stay and tend the goats. And I will take care of you." For ten years I stayed with the old woman and I came to love her as if she were my own mother. I had to spend one of my silver coins to buy a few things to make her last years happier. I wept when finally she died. By now I was twenty-two and a grown man, but still I yearned to go to Jerusalem and find the one who was born to be King of the Jews.

Off I set again, this time on a horse I had obtained in trade for the goats. Over mountains and across rivers I traveled on my way. One day, as I was fording a small stream, suddenly I was surrounded by ferocious-looking armed men. They pulled me off my horse and, with a sword to my throat, demanded: "Are you not an official of the hated King Darius?"

"No," I protested, "I am only an apprentice wise man." And I told them my story.

"We apologize for our mistake," they said. "King Darius has invaded our land and enslaved our people. We are guerrilla fighters, pledged to win back our people's freedom. We are sorry; you may go." I mounted my horse and was about to set off when I heard a moan from a tent set back a way in the trees. I rode over and looked in. The tent was full of wounded soldiers – no doctor, no medicine, not even beds to lie on.

What could I do? I wanted to get to Jerusalem but I could not leave these people to suffer. The wise men had taught me something of medicine and how to care for the sick – I had to stay. For ten years I was doctor to the guerrilla army. I even had to spend my second silver piece to buy medicine. Finally the war of liberation was over. The people were free and I could go on my way.

Off I set again for Jerusalem to find the one born to be King of the Jews. But only two weeks later I caught up with a man carrying a baby and leading two young children by the hand. Wearily they trudged along the dusty road. "What has happened, sir?" I asked. "Why are you all alone with these children on the edge of the desert?"

(continued on the next page)

The Fourth Wise Man (*continued*)

"My name is Nuko," the man replied. "We were moving to a new town when our caravan was attacked by fierce desert raiders. We hid in a ravine. Many of our people were killed. All our belongings were stolen and my wife was carried off into slavery. We are going to look for her. We cannot leave her in slavery!"

"I will come with you and help with the children while you search," I said. So I did.

For ten years we searched and we came to love each other very much. Finally, one day, in the marketplace of a strange town, we came upon a slave auction. You can imagine our joy when we saw Nuko's wife on the auction platform. I bought her freedom with my last piece of silver. But it was worth it, and more, to see the happiness of that family. With tears of joy and sadness I said good-bye and set off again on my journey. Still I must find the one I was looking for; still I must find the King of the Jews.

Finally I came to Jerusalem. It was springtime and the leaves on the trees, the flowers, the fresh green grass, were very beautiful. There was a festival in progress. I think they called it "Passover." As soon as I entered the city I asked the first person I came to: "Where is the King of the Jews?"

"We have no king," he answered angrily. "We are ruled by those blankety-blank Romans," and he spat in disgust.

"You must mean one of those messiah types," another said. "They're worse than the Romans – full of false promises, getting us all excited over nothing."

"I think they are crowning a king of the Jews right now," a third man said. "Go out through the north gate to Skull Hill. You'll find the King of the Jews on his throne, all right!" and he laughed in an ugly sort of way.

Through the city I went, out the north gate until I came to a bare, rocky hill. There, to my horror, I found three men hanging, each on a cross. Over the center cross was a sign which read: "Here is the King of the Jews." I couldn't believe my eyes, that people could be so cruel. Closer I went, up to the feet of the dying man. Then, as I looked at him, his eyes opened. They were so full of suffering, and yet so full of love. I knew...I knew that   I had found the one I had been searching for.

"Lord, I have come too late," I cried. "Foolishly I have wasted my time; foolishly I have wasted my money. If only I had my three pieces of silver left I could buy you down off this cross!"

He looked at me and whispered: "You are not too late, my child. Remember the old woman and her goats, remember the wounded guerrilla fighters, remember Nuko, his children, his wife in slavery. Everything you did for the least of these my sisters and brothers, you did for me. Understand that, and you are wise indeed. You have given the greatest gift of all: not frankincense, not gold, not myrrh. You have given yourself to those who hurt; you have given yourself to me!"

From *Celebrating the Church Year Intergenerationally* by Thomas Harding, Enthusia Enterprises. Used by permission.

Section C: Season after Epiphany

Mood and Flavor of the Season

The Feast of the Epiphany on January 6 marks the end of the Christmas Season. It is the transition to the Epiphany Season, also known as the Sundays or Season after Epiphany. There may be as few as four or as many as nine Sundays in this season, depending on the date of Easter and the beginning of Lent. The first Sunday after Epiphany is the Baptism of Our Lord. The season ends with Shrove Tuesday.

The word "epiphany" means "showing forth" or "manifestation." During this season, we see God's glory and purpose "made manifest" through the life and teachings of Jesus. The mood is one of proclamation and growth. The liturgical color for the first Sunday (the Baptism of Our Lord) and for the last Sunday (Transfiguration) is white, symbolizing days of special significance. Otherwise the color of this season is green, symbolizing growth.

During the Season after Epiphany, the gospel readings focus on the call of the disciples, and the teaching and healing ministry of Jesus. Traditionally, this is a time when the Church focuses on its "call" and mission in the world. With his baptism, Jesus began to take specific action in response to God's call. God also summons us, both as individuals and as a people. God's call to us is not something we hear with our ear, but something we feel with our hearts. The lectionary passages for the last Sunday of the Season after Epiphany (Transfiguration) describe a mystical event experienced by Jesus and his followers. These readings provide a unique opportunity for youth to explore their own "awesome" experiences of God.

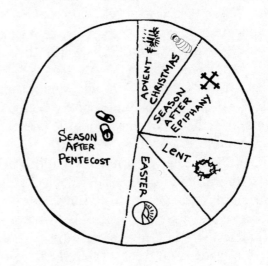

Special Days

The special days in this season reflect the themes of "call" and mission. January 15 marks the anniversary of the birth of civil rights' activist Martin Luther King, Jr. February marks Black History Month. Many churches observe the Week of Prayer for Christian Unity, held in the week that includes the Feast of the Conversion of Saint Paul on January 25. February 14 is the feast day of Saint Valentine, who was imprisoned and put to death for being a Christian.

Just prior to Ash Wednesday, Canadian churches focus on global concerns and mission projects through the program of Ten Days for Global Justice (formerly Ten Days for World Development). During this season, check with your church to learn about your denomination's mission education programs.

The Season after Epiphany ends with Shrove Tuesday. The word "shrove" comes from the verb "to shrive," meaning to confess and receive absolution (God's forgiveness). Shrove Tuesday precedes Ash Wednesday (the first day of the Season of Lent). Early Christians prepared for fasting or eating simple food in Lent by using up the last of foods like eggs, sugar, and milk. This began the tradition of eating pancakes for Shrove Tuesday dinner (a simple way to use up the eggs, milk, and sugar in the house). Today we often refer to this day as "Pancake Tuesday." Some churches combine the feasting with an Ash Wednesday celebration after sundown on Tuesday.

In some places around the world, these preparations are part of "Mardi Gras" ("Fat Tuesday") or "Carnival" – a time when people indulge in parties, costumes, and good food. The word "carnival" comes from the Latin "carnem levare," meaning "the putting away of meat." Since early Christians would "give up" eating meat and other rich foods during Lent, both Mardi Gras and Carnival were seen as a last chance to celebrate before a period of restraint. The real reason for all the indulgence and revelry is often lost in the modern-day context, but these traditions do originate from early church tradition.

Implications for Youth Ministry

The themes of "call" and discipleship in the Season after Epiphany are important ones for youth. Like Jesus at the time of his baptism, adolescents are sorting out their identities and discerning the "paths" they will follow. Today's youth test boundaries, sort out values, search for their "real" selves, and struggle with important decisions about the future. For adolescents this can be both liberating and frightening.

Statistics show that, by age fifteen, 80% of those who will leave the church have already left – an astounding fact when you think of its implications for youth ministry. Youth are at an age when questioning is very important in their faith development. This often includes questioning the role of the church and faith in their day-to-day

lives. Youth groups need to be supportive and accepting places where youth can ask their questions and talk about new-found insights. According to research done by Reginald Bibby and Donald Posterski (*Teen Trends: A Nation in Motion*), nearly 60% of the surveyed teens indicated they have spiritual needs and 25% said that spirituality is "very important" to them. Some youth have a very strong sense of God's "call" in their lives while others have difficulty recognizing they've ever had an experience of God. Some express doubts about God's presence in their lives at all. According to Bibby and Posterski's research, 81% of teens say they believe in the existence of God and 34% believe they have had an experience of God.

After the Christmas rush, this slower season may be ideal for having a sleep-over. Youth can experience living in community and reflect on what it meant for Jesus and his disciples. Organize a viewing of a movie about miracles, the supernatural, or about someone like Rosa Parks or Martin Luther King, Jr., who "lived out their faith" through their actions. The group might also enjoy hosting a Shrove Tuesday pancake supper to raise money for a retreat or outreach project (see **Celebrations for Mardi Gras and Shrove Tuesday** on page 103).

"Call"

Group Check-in

Sit in a circle to make a **Friendship Web**. Ask someone to begin the check-in and hand them the ball of yarn. Invite them to briefly describe one thing they did over the past week and then, holding on to the end, toss the ball of yarn to another person in the group. Then that person shares something about their week, holds on to a section of yarn, and tosses the ball to another group member, and so on until everyone has had a turn. (*Note:* You may carefully pick up the web at the end of the check-in and tack it to a wall or bulletin board as a reminder of the group's "connectedness.")

Being Called

These exercises can introduce a discussion about the ways God calls us in our ordinary lives.

- **Telephone.** Try this old standby with a simple message like "God calls each one of us." Gather in a circle. Whisper the message in the ear of the person next to you and invite them to pass the message on to the next person. See what message you end up with.
- **Silly Instructions.** Ahead of time, on slips of paper write instructions like "Stand on a chair and yell 'The British are coming!'" or "Laugh like Dracula" or "Ask everyone in the group if they've seen your Bible." The instructions should be a little silly, but fun. Hand out an instruction slip to each group member. On your count, have everyone unfold theirs, read it and do what it instructs them to do.

Afterwards use these questions as discussion starters:

1. How did everyone respond?
2. How did you feel (e.g. surprised, embarrassed, confused)?
3. Did anyone feel reluctant or refuse to do what their instructions asked?
4. How might this exercise be similar to the way people experience God's call?

Busy Signal Drama

Begin by brainstorming: What can happen when you call someone on the telephone? (e.g. busy signal, answering machine, person could hang up on you, enthusiastic response) In pairs or small groups, have group members create skits that explore one of these happening when God calls them. How do they see themselves, and teenagers in general, responding to God's call? What is God asking them to do?

Paper Bag Skits

The Bible is full of stories about people who received a call from God. Some didn't understand it at first, others were reluctant or refused to do what God called them to do. Drama can help us discover some of these Bible stories.

You will need: several paper bags with five or six randomly chosen items in each, such as a wooden spoon, table cloth, magazine, earring, road map, etc.

Instructions: Divide into small groups. Ask each group to look up a different Bible story (see examples at top of next page) and read it together. Give each group one of the paper bags you prepared. Explain that they must use all of these items and all of the members of the group to present the story they just read. Allow enough time for them to create their skits and then present them.

Bible Stories about God's Call

Exodus 3:1-12   1 Samuel 3:1-21
Jeremiah 1:4-10   Jonah 1:1-17
Ezekiel 1:28-2:7

God's Call

Read some Bible stories about God's call (see above). Who experienced God's call? How and where did they experience it? (e.g. through a dream, through a strange and new experience, alone, with others) How did the people in the stories respond?

How do you think God speaks to people today? Have you ever had an experience like those described in these stories – a strange dream, something unexpected that changed the way you saw something, a powerful experience, a gentle "nudge"? Invite group members to talk with a partner about an experience they've had. Ask them to discuss this question: If this were a call from God, what might God be trying to tell you?

(Some youth may not be sure if they've ever heard a call or had an experience of God. Assure them that often we do not realize the importance of experiences and events until much later.)

Closing Worship

Related Scripture Passages: Romans 10:11-13, 1 Corinthians 1:26-31
Story: Tell the story **Called to the Mountain Top** (see next page).
Meditation: Darken the room, if possible, and do the following guided meditation.

Guided Meditation

(Invite youth to get into a comfortable position, close their eyes, and concentrate on their breathing for a few minutes. As you read the meditation, pause after each sentence to allow the youth to reflect on what you are saying.)

Imagine that God is directing a film about your life. In the first scene, you are very young. Picture yourself as a young child. What were some of the special things you remember from your childhood? Trips you took? Holidays? Special people? Where is God in this scene? What did God call you to do? In the second scene, you are in your teens. Picture yourself as you are. What are some of the things happening in your life now? What are your hopes and dreams? Who are the special people in your life? Where is God in this scene? How is God calling you now? In the final scene of the movie, you are older. Picture yourself in the future. What will the rest of the film look like? Where do you hope to be? What might you be doing? Where will God be in that scene? What do you think God is calling you to do and to be?

(After a few minutes, invite the youth to slowly come back to the present. Invite them to open their eyes when they are ready.)

Called to the Mountain Top – The Story of Martin Luther King, Jr.

Martin Luther King, Jr. was born on January 15, 1929. Growing up in Atlanta, Georgia, Martin's best friends had been 2 brothers, Jim and Bill, whose parents owned a store in their neighborhood. Martin, Jim, and Bill were almost inseparable – until one day when Martin was about 7 years old. He remembers going to Jim and Bill's house; their mother met Martin at the door and told him that her boys couldn't come out and play with Martin – not that day, or ever again. In tears, Martin ran all the way home.

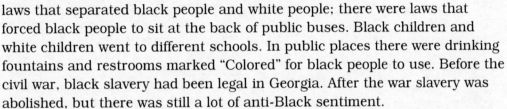

When Martin asked his mother why Jim and Bill's mother wouldn't allow the boys to play together anymore, she explained that it was because he was black and his friends were white. At that time, in the United States, there were laws that separated black people and white people; there were laws that forced black people to sit at the back of public buses. Black children and white children went to different schools. In public places there were drinking fountains and restrooms marked "Colored" for black people to use. Before the civil war, black slavery had been legal in Georgia. After the war slavery was abolished, but there was still a lot of anti-Black sentiment.

Martin was profoundly affected by this experience. He had been raised believing that God had created all people equal. Martin knew that the laws that discriminated against people on the basis of color didn't fit with God's plan for our world, and he believed that the laws had to be changed.

As he grew, Martin saw more clearly that this was his purpose – his "calling" from God. Martin got involved in the Black Civil Rights Movement of the 1960s. He became a powerful speaker, a symbol of hope for many people. On April 4, 1968, the day after he delivered a speech to thousands of people in Memphis, Tennessee, Dr. King was shot and killed.

Witnessing

"Actions speak louder than words"

Whether we realize it or not, we are modeling our faith to others every day of our lives. In the things we say and in the way we act, in the choices we make every day as we attempt to live in "Christ-like" ways, all say a lot to the people around us. If our values are rooted in our faith, then the way we live will reflect that. We must not forget that our actions – choosing to recycle, caring for others, taking part in a peace demonstration, sharing our money with others who have less, choosing not to buy war-toys – express our faith in Christ, too.

Wearing Your Witness

"We as Christians can promote the gospel of Jesus Christ through expressing our faith on clothing," reads one catalog advertisement for Christian T-shirts. Wearing clothing with a Christian message on it (or having a bumper-sticker on your car, a poster on your bedroom wall, etc.) is one way some people like to convey a message to others about who they are and what they believe.

Church Publications

Most churches today have a variety of publications – informational pamphlets, a church magazine. These can be ways to spread the Christian message, too! Some churches make their publications available by placing them in public places or doing mass-mailings. Other church publications may be subscribed to by church members, but often libraries will keep copies on file for the public's use.

Television Broadcasting

VISION TV is unique in the world as a specialty cable network reaching over 5.5 million homes across Canada. Its mandate is to portray the strength and integrity of Canada's religious and cultural heritages, and provide an alternative national television service which emphasizes spiritual, ethical and moral values. Many Christian denominations as well as other faith groups purchase airtime in order to reach people with their messages and their stories.

Walk for Jesus

Another way some people like to express their Christian faith is by attending events like the annual "Walk for Jesus." Once a year, on the same day, Christians around the world take to the streets to "stand up and be counted" as followers of Jesus. In some places, like Brazil, the walk has attracted hundreds of thousands of people each year.

Bible Society/Gideons

There are over 105 national Bible Society offices around the world. Each year, the Bible Society distributes millions of Bibles, published in 75 different languages in Canada alone, as well as assisting in translation, publication and distribution to some 150 countries throughout the world. The Bible Society's goal is to help share the good news by providing copies of the Bible at affordable prices. The Gideons are another well-known group – their goal is to provide Bibles free of charge so that they are available to everyone. You know the copies of the Bibles you almost always find in hotel rooms? Yep, those are supplied by the Gideons.

"Streetcorner Witnessing"

Some churches like to share their message with others directly face to face. They like to engage people where they are – on the streetcorner, outside of the supermarket, as they go about their day-to-day lives.

Living Compassion

Some people like to take the good news to people in "bad news" places. One such group is "The Bridge," an ecumenical group in Brampton, Ontario, that makes a direct link between inmates in correctional institutions and the outside community. Volunteers are trained to work with groups "inside" the prison system and with groups of ex-prisoners who are trying to make it on the "outside" as well. The groups offer a chance for real communication and healing which, volunteers say, happens as much for them as for those inmates they go to help. Here witnessing to the "good news" is as much by deed as by words. As their brochure says, they "provide you with a challenge worthy of the name Christian."

Idea Page #2

Witness

Group Check-in

If you had to come up with a newspaper headline to sum up something that happened in your life last week, what would it be? The headline might reflect something interesting you did, something that really had an effect on you, or some good news you've received. Ask for a volunteer to begin and then everyone takes a turn. (For example, they might want to say something like this: "Extra! Extra! Read all about it...Girl, 15, Wins Battle with Quadratic Equations.")

Witnessing

The word apostle means "one sent out." In a way, we are all apostles – ones sent out to share the good news of Jesus with others. What are some of the ways you know that people share the Christian message? List everyone's ideas on newsprint.

Hand out copies of **Witnessing** on page 90. Look it over together. How many of these ways did the group name? Are there ways of witnessing that you had never thought of? How do you share your faith with others? How does the church share its faith? In which ways would you feel comfortable "witnessing"? Why do you think it's important to "witness" your beliefs to others?

Witness Scenario

See the game **Witness Scenario** on pages 94-96 for instructions and game cards.

Either/Or

This exercise invites participants to choose between two options, each time choosing the one that appeals to them the most. It encourages personal connection, imagination, and symbolic thinking. Clear the room so everyone can move easily. Ask the following questions – each has two alternatives. After each, invite those who choose the first option to go to one side of the room and those who choose the second option to go to the other side. Encourage people to go with their first impulse and not spend too much time thinking. After each choice, ask everyone for the reason behind their choices.

As followers of Jesus, is it most important for us:

1. a) to know each other as individuals?
   OR
   b) to hear God's Word?

2. a) to know each other as individuals?
   OR
   b) to know and be responsive to the needs of society?

3. a) to tell others about Jesus Christ?
   OR
   b) to practice what we preach?

4. a) to practice what we preach?
   OR
   b) to examine what we believe?

5. a) to know and be responsive to the needs of society?
   OR
   b) to tell others about Jesus Christ?

After completing the exercise, gather together to talk about the experience. What choices were easy? What ones were difficult? Were you ever almost alone on one side of the room? How did that feel? Did others' reasons for choosing (or not choosing) a statement make you think differently? How is each of these a way of "witnessing"? How do you witness to others?

Evangelization

Ask someone to read aloud the information box on this page describing the origin and meanings of the word "evangelization." Share the information from the graph. Then discuss the questions below in small groups.

- According to the graph, what are the most likely ways people will become involved in a church?
- What kinds of things do you think "personal witness" involves? What might we do (as individuals, as a church) to provide personal witness to others?
- How much evangelization do you think Christians should be doing? In what ways do you think it should be done? How important is it to attract new members to the church?
- Do you think welcoming others is a form of evangelizing? What good news is being shared?
- What makes you feel welcome in a group? What would convince you to join? What makes you feel welcome here at church? What kinds of things do you think attract young people to the church?

Marketing the Church

Imagine you are members of a marketing firm that has just been hired by the church to come up with a scheme for attracting new members. Brainstorm ideas. Include "market research" to find out what attracts people of different ages to the church. Then proceed to consider how these interests and needs can be met, how the church can advertise, and what good news is being shared by these "new and improved features." Let your imaginations run wild!

"Evangelization" comes from the Greek verb euangelizomai meaning "to proclaim good news or the gospel." The Apostle Paul used euangelizomai primarily as a missionary term. It had the simple meaning of "announcing the good news of Jesus" as well as the broader meaning that described "the whole activity of a Christian disciple."

The word "evangelize" has a very different meaning for many people today. By the seventeenth century "evangelize" meant "to win over to the Christian faith." Today, the first things that come to mind for many when they hear the word are the "televangelists" on TV. Many of these people are well-known for their charismatic, fist-pounding preaching about the Bible. They still try to evangelize in the original sense of the word, but also in the sense of the seventeenth century evangelizers who were perhaps more concerned with "converting" people to a particular faith.

From its history, these three things can be said about evangelization past and present:

1. Evangelization, which can take many forms, is focused on "sharing faith."
2. Evangelization has a strong missionary focus – both in the sense that means sharing faith with non-believers and in the sense of promoting a broad range of Christian activities.
3. Evangelization as we know it today is a "new" word for an old reality. Christians have always shared their faith, even if they have used other words to describe this.

How People Get Involved in Church

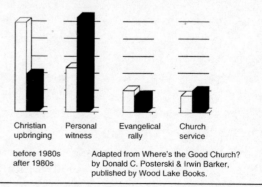

| Christian upbringing | Personal witness | Evangelical rally | Church service |

before 1980s
after 1980s

Adapted from *Where's the Good Church?* by Donald C. Posterski & Irwin Barker, published by Wood Lake Books.

Closing Worship

Related Scripture Passages: Matthew 28:16-20, 1 John 5:10a,11
Prayer: Read together the litany **Spreading the Good News** on the next page.

Spreading the Good News

Invite everyone to say the litany response "...hear our prayer"
and invite four volunteers to be the four Readers.

Reader #1: Let those who have received the good news remember those messengers of God's truth and love who have been imprisoned in an attempt to silence the message. We think of the many adults, children, and teenagers around the world who have been arrested, detained, even tortured and killed for speaking against the evil they have experienced. O God, give them strength and courage. God of justice, love, and mercy...

ALL: ...hear our prayer.

Reader #2: We pray for the many "disappeared" priests, students and parents who have been seized by the governments of El Salvador, Guatemala, Nicaragua, and Argentina in an attempt to silence their cry for justice. We pray for the children and youth on the streets of Brazil who are barely surviving, and who live in fear of being captured by the army and killed simply because they are an "embarrassment" and "bad for tourism." O God, give them strength and courage. God of justice, love, and mercy...

ALL: ...hear our prayer.

Reader #3: We also pray for young people in our own country – runaways, those caught in the web of drugs or alcohol, gang violence, family violence, and those with no attentive adult to hear them. We pray for those who feel alone and those who do not experience the good news of God's love and acceptance in their daily lives. God of justice, love, and mercy...

ALL: ...hear our prayer.

Reader #4: Forgive us, God, for taking our freedom and your message of love and justice so lightly. Help us find the ways to live out our faith and to spread the good news to others in our speaking, hearing, and living. God of justice, love, and mercy...

ALL: ...hear our prayer. Amen.

Witness Scenario

Instructions: Make a copy of these pages and the **Answer Cards** on page 96. Mount on cardboard backing if you wish, and cut apart. This game is played like Scruples™. The object of the game is to get rid of your witness scenario cards. Each player is dealt only one answer card, face down so others can't see it. Deal out two or more witness scenario cards (depending on the size of your group) to each member of the group. Moving clockwise from the dealer, the first player chooses one of their scenario questions to ask any other player. Ask someone you think will respond with the same answer as the answer card you have in your hand. If you get the answer you were looking for, you may discard the scenario card. No matter how the person responds, discard your answer card and select a new one each turn.

✂ *cut apart on lines*

Would you wear a T-shirt with a Christian message printed on it?

Would you give half of your allowance each week as your offering (to the church)?

Would you attend a Christian youth conference?

Would you take part in a religious drama touring schools and churches?

Would you hand out information on the street corner about your church (e.g. when services are held, what programs are available)?

Would you stand up for someone who is being picked on for being "different"?

Would you choose to boycott a product that was made in a country where workers are paid low wages, in order to make a statement to the company that makes the product?

Would you send a card or owers to someone you knew was feeling down-in-the-dumps?

Would you help out at a dinner for homeless people?

Would you baby-sit free-of-charge for someone you knew couldn't really afford to pay you?

Witness Scenario

Would you go to a concert of contemporary Christian music?

Would you challenge someone who is making racial or prejudicial remarks?

Would you say something to a friend you observed littering?

Would you give a copy of the Bible away as a birthday, graduation or "in sympathy" gift?

Would you invite a friend from school who doesn't normally attend church to come to a meeting of your youth group (or attend church with you some Sunday)?

Would you help out with a church fund raiser instead of going somewhere with your friends on a Friday night?

Would you readily admit to being a member of a church if the group of people you were with at the time were making fun of people who go to church?

Would you say grace before a meal in a public restaurant if it was usual for you to give thanks before eating?

Would you talk to a friend about your Christian beliefs?

Would you choose not to listen to a particular kind of music or group if you thought its music gave out poor messages?

Answer Cards

Instructions: You will need these cards to play the game **Witness Scenario** on the previous pages and the game **Choices Scenario** on page 114. Photocopy this page, mount on cardboard backing if you wish, and cut apart the squares.

✂ *cut apart on lines*

YES	YES	YES	YES
NO	NO	NO	NO
YES	YES	YES	YES
NO	NO	NO	NO
DEPENDS	DEPENDS	DEPENDS	DEPENDS
DEPENDS	DEPENDS	DEPENDS	DEPENDS

Idea Page #3

Prisoners' Day and St. Valentine's Day

Group Check-in

Invite everyone to think of one word to describe how they're feeling today. Then ask them to greet the other group members with a handshake and an exchange of one-word descriptions.

Criminal Justice Speaker or Film

In some denominations, the Sunday nearest February 14 is designated Criminal Justice Sunday or Prisoners' Sunday. Without taking away the importance of celebrating human relationships, on this day we can learn about and remember those who are imprisoned.

• Invite a prison chaplain or someone from an organization that works with people in prison or ex-prisoners (e.g. the John Howard or Elizabeth Fry Society). Ask them to speak to the group about their work, how it has made a difference to their lives, and how their faith has influenced their choice to work with prisoners.

• Invite a member of a local chapter of **Amnesty International** to talk about advocacy work on behalf of prisoners of conscience (see box on next page).

• Watch a film that focuses on prisoners such as "Cry Freedom" (the story of black activist Steven Biko), "In the Name of the Father," or an educational film that examines the prison and justice system. (See **Videos and Youth Groups** on page 14.)

Prisoners in Our Society

We learn about the criminal justice system from the media, from our own experiences, and from the experiences of others. What do you know about the criminal justice system? How do you view prisoners? How does society view prisoners? Plan a "first-hand" experience of the criminal justice system (e.g. take part in a worship service at a correctional facility, visit a rehabilitation center for young offenders, write letters to prisoners of conscience).

The Story of Saint Valentine

This story happened about 300 years after Jesus was born, when Christianity as a religion was in its infancy. It was extremely dangerous then to be a member of this faith that said Christ was a more important authority than the Roman Emperor. The Emperor, of course, expected the people to follow him. Indeed, he was widely considered to be a god himself.

A priest named Valentine was put in jail for being a follower of Jesus and refusing to worship the Emperor. Valentine was very lonely and sad, suspecting – rightly – that he was going to be put to death. The jailer's daughter saw him, however, and felt compassion for him. She began to visit him and sometimes she brought him food.

When Valentine learned that his death was imminent, he wrote a beautiful note to his young friend, thanking her for her kindness and signed it "Your Valentine." This probably was what began the tradition of sending cards to loved ones on St. Valentine's day.

St. Valentine's gesture had deeper meaning than an expression of personal affection. His life and death upheld the right of individuals to act according to their consciences and deeply held beliefs. The girl's actions symbolize the strength that friendship and compassion give to those resisting injustice.

If it wasn't for the courage and faith of early Christians like Valentine, the Christian church we are a part of today may never have survived.

Amnesty International

Youth leaders may wish to become members of Amnesty International through the "Teacher's Network" which allows you to receive the *AI Bulletin* and *Teachers' Network Newsletter* containing materials especially for older children and youth. Send $25 (suggested contribution) indicating "Teacher's Network Membership" to:

Human Rights Educators' Network
Amnesty International
53 W. Jackson, Ste. 1162
Chicago, IL 60604

Amnesty International
Canadian Section
214 Montreal Rd., Suite 401
Vanier, ON   K1L 9Z9

St. Valentine's Event

Here are some ideas for planning an intergenerational event on this theme:

- Have a potluck dinner. Invite a prison chaplain or member of an organization like the John Howard or Elizabeth Fry Society to speak after the meal about their work meeting the spiritual needs of those in prison or jail.
- Dramatize **The Story of St. Valentine** (see box on previous page).
- Make **Simple Sugar Cookies** (page 100) and cards telling the story of St. Valentine for prisoners. Ask a prison chaplain or member of a prisoner support organization to deliver these to a local correctional facility or prison. Sign the cards from "Your Valentine."
- Organize a fund-raising soup, sandwich, and sundae luncheon to raise money for prison outreach program.

Closing Worship

Related Scripture Passages: Matthew 25:31-40, Luke 3:16-21, Acts 16:16-34

Prayer: *Print the response "Have mercy on us" on newsprint. Ask a volunteer to be the Reader.*

Reader: Creator God, we recognize that our world is not as you would have it. You created us to be free, to love and care for one another and for creation. But all too often we fail. Loving God...

Response: Have mercy on us.

Reader: O God, we are dismayed at our overflowing prisons and jails, our soaring crime rates, growing violence. We build bigger and bigger prisons to house those we deem unfit for society. We talk about "cleaning up the streets" and "getting tough on crime." We have contempt, not compassion, for wrongdoers. Loving God...

Response: Have mercy on us.

Reader: Compassionate God, help us not to forget that your son, too, was once called a criminal – found guilty, handcuffed and stripped, treated roughly by guards, humiliated. Help us to see in the faces of criminals, our brothers and sisters, to see that we have been quick to judge and slow to have compassion, Loving God...

Response: Have mercy on us.

Reader: Forgiving God, when you were dying on the cross you forgave those who hated and despised you, those who were responsible for your death, setting before us an example of how we must be with one another. Yet our hearts are often too hard to forgive and we are convinced that we are justified in not forgiving. Loving God...

Response: Have mercy on us.

Reader: Help us, God, to see what you would have us do. Amen.

Idea Page #4

Love

Group Check-in

Tom Hanks' Forrest Gump coined the phrase "Life is like a box of chocolates – you never know what you're goin' to get." Ask everyone to take turns describing how they feel about the past week by comparing it to a kind of chocolate (e.g. Last week was like those chocolates that come wrapped in tinfoil – hard to get into it and frustrating).

Reverse Musical Chairs

This is the familiar game with a new twist that's bound to bring the group closer! Arrange chairs back to back in a single line, making sure there is one for everyone. Play some music (preferably love songs) and invite everyone to dance around the chairs. When the music stops, everyone claims a chair. Then remove a chair or two, start the music again and when the music stops everyone claims a seat. Some group members will have to sit on others' laps. Continue taking away chairs until you have just one or two left – with the whole group on them!

Journaling about Love

Provide paper, folders, and pens to make journals. For today's entry, suggest group members complete some of the following sentences:
• When I love someone I...
• The most loving thing a person can do is...
• I feel God's love when...
• I feel loved by my family when...
• I feel unloved by my family when...
Encourage everyone to generate additional sentences about love and relationships. See **Lenten Journaling** on page 124 for other ideas.

Celebrate Together!

Planning and enjoying celebrations bring people closer together. Plan a group or congregational celebration for the season. (See **Celebrations for Mardi Gras and Shrove Tuesday** on page 103-104.)

Love Songs

Ahead of time, invite group members to bring cassette tapes of some popular love songs. Listen to some of these and discuss their lyrics. Use the questions in the box below for discussion starters.

> 1. How would you describe the type of love expressed in each song? For example, is it romantic, platonic, jealous, unhealthy, "true," mature, "fairytale-ish," consuming, superficial?
> 2. What feelings are associated with love in this song?
> 3. What images are associated with love in this song?
> 4. Do you think love songs, in general, express "true" relationships and feelings?

Songs of Praise

Together read some of the Psalms or a section of the Song of Songs (Song of Solomon) in the Bible.

The Book of Psalms is the ancient hymnbook and prayer book of the Hebrew people, a collection of sacred songs and prayers that often describe the loving relationship between God and the people.

The Song of Songs is a collection of love poems that has often been interpreted by Jews as describing not a human relationship but the relationship between God and God's people, and by Christians as a description of the relationship between Christ and the Church.

Use the questions in the box on this page to discuss the images and feelings presented by these songs and poems.

Loving Affirmations

Cut large heart shapes out of red construction paper so there's one for everyone. Cut out enough smaller hearts so that each group member has one for each of the other group members. Invite them to write their names on the front of the large heart. On the smaller hearts, ask them to write something they appreciate or like about each member of the group. Hand out lengths of string. Have everyone attach one end to the back of their large heart using tape or a stapler so that it hangs down. Then place these in the center of the circle. Attach the smaller hearts to the strings so that each person will end up with a string of hearts affirming them and their contributions to the group.

The Greatest Commandment

Read Matthew 22:34-40. What does it mean to love God "with all your heart, with all your soul and with all your mind"? What prevents people from loving God or loving others? What prevents people from loving God, themselves, or others?

Hand out current newspapers, news magazines, blank paper, and pencils. Ask everyone to draw or find pictures, headlines, or articles that symbolize these barriers. Ask them to explain the symbols they chose.

Have a Heart!

Make these cookies to share with the congregation after the worship service or at a special celebration:

Simple Sugar Cookies
1 1/2 cups (375mL) icing sugar
1 cup (250mL) margarine (softened)
2 1/2 cups (625mL) all-purpose flour
1/2 tsp. (2mL) almond extract
1 tsp. (5mL) cream of tartar
1 tsp. (5mL) baking soda
1 tsp. (5mL) vanilla
1 egg

Mix sugar, margarine, almond extract, egg and vanilla. Stir in flour, soda and cream of tartar. Refrigerate 3 hr. before using. Divide the dough into several balls and roll these out on a well-floured surface approx. 1/4in. (5mm) thick. Cut with heart-shaped cutter. Bake at 375°F (190°C) for 7-8 min. Decorate when cool with pink icing, sprinkles, cinnamon hearts, etc.

Closing Worship

Related Scripture Passages: Matt. 22:36-40, John 13:34-35, 1 John 3:11,17-18, 1 Cor.13
Meditation: Draw, or cut out of news magazines, pictures and words symbolizing barriers to loving one another and God. (Use the symbols from the **Greatest Commandment** above, if you did it.) Create a collage on a large sheet of newsprint with all the symbols. Look at it in silence then ask a volunteer to read the prayer.
Prayer: Loving God, we confess that too often we fail to live out the commandment
Jesus gave us to love one another.
We live in a society that encourages us to compete with one another, to judge and be judged, to "look out for number one."
We struggle to have a positive self-image in a society that tells us there is always some way to make ourselves better.
We confess that we have not loved you, our neighbors, or ourselves, in the way you intended.
Help us to love more and try more to create a loving and just world. Amen.

Idea Page #5 Seasonal Celebrations

Group Check-in

Divide into pairs and ask partners to talk about (1) the best gift they've ever received and (2) the best gift they've ever given. Ask two pairs to form a group of four and have youth tell the rest of the group what their partner's best gifts received and given were. Hand out sheets of newsprint and a marker to each group. Have them divide their page into two columns. Ask them to spend a few minutes brainstorming the gifts they think youth have to offer to the church and the gifts the church has to offer youth.

Season after Epiphany Party

Some groups enjoy a special event to mark the first gathering after the Christmas break. Others like to plan an event to beat the "winter blahs." Here are some ideas:

- Plan an outing to a swimming pool, bowling alley, skating rink, or toboggan hill. Send out invitations by mail. Encourage everyone to bring friends.
- Plan a candle-lit dinner or candle-lit board games night.
- Plan to take part in, or create your own, midwinter celebration incorporating rituals from **Other Midwinter Celebrations** on the next page, or **Celebrations for Mardi Gras and Shrove Tuesday** (see page 103-104.)

Midwinter Video or TV Night

Get together in a member's home to see a movie. Or hold a favorite TV program marathon. Plan ahead – ask members to tape episodes of their favorite TV programs and bring them along.

Shrove Tuesday Event

Plan an intergenerational or fund-raising event for your church. See **Celebrations for Mardi Gras and Shrove Tuesday** on page 103-104 and **Shrove Tuesday or Ash Wednesday Service** in Section F.

Group Time Line

On a 4 ft. (1.3m) piece of banner paper create a Time Line from September to May (or whenever your group is likely to end for the year). Write or draw symbols of things you've done together since the beginning of the year. Do the same for any events, retreats or projects that you are planning for the rest of the year (e.g. windup retreat).

Tape the Time Line to a wall. Invite group members to add to it. Write evaluatory remarks or draw pictures on it near the activities you've already done. Write suggestions or draw pictures suggesting things you would like to do in the remainder of the year. Afterwards, talk about all the ideas and responses.

If you had a brainstorming session at the beginning of the year, compare these "have done" and "want to do" lists. For example, if you talked about doing service projects at the beginning of the year but haven't done one yet, is this now a priority? Is there a need for more variety in the types of activities? (e.g. social, group discussion, participating in worship) Get ideas from group members and formulate some plans.

Alternatively, try the **Community Links** on page 34.

Dragon's Tail (Chuo Tung Wei)

Divide into teams of about eight. Have teams form lines, with people placing hands on the shoulders or hips of the person in front. The first person in line is the dragon's head; the last person is the dragon's tail. The challenge is to see if the Dragon's Head can catch the Dragon's Tail. Everyone counts: "Em (one), er (two), san (three), ko (go)!" On "ko" the dragon's body moves together as the Head reaches out to grab the Tail. If the Head succeeds or the body breaks apart, the Head becomes the new Tail and the person next in line takes over as the new Head.

Birth Year

List the birth years of group members and research information on the Chinese year coinciding with each (i.e. Year of the Rat, Year of the Dog). Have an "unbirthday" party to celebrate everyone's birthday at once.

Other Midwinter Celebrations

Chinese New Year (beginning in late January)
The Chinese New Year begins on the first day of the second new moon after the winter solstice. It is a celebration of the new year and of each person's birthday. Traditionally, this most important festival of the Chinese year lasted for a whole month, and included feasts, games, firecrackers and visiting one's friends and family. During the visits, children receive sweetened rice cakes – as round as the family circle is round, and as sweet as peace. All the treats of the season symbolize happiness, peace, and life. The new year is a time to say good-bye to the old year and greet the new. It is considered important to settle quarrels so that everyone can begin the new year anew.

Ramadan (beginning in February)
During the month of Ramadan, Muslims around the world pray and fast. Ramadan recalls the Prophet Mohammed's month of fasting and prayer as he waited for Allah to tell him how he and his people should live. Muslims eat and drink nothing from sunrise to sunset each day during Ramadan.

Eed-ul-Fitr, known as the festival of the fast breaking, marks the end of Ramadan. On the eve of Eed-ul-Fitr, everyone looks for the new moon. When they see it, everyone shouts for joy and offers praise to Allah. In Islamic countries, Eed-ul-Fitr is marked by drums and cannons. Before the fast ends, everyone must give something to the poor. Then the fast ends and the party begins. People give presents, they dress in new clothes, greet one another with holiday wishes, hold family get-togethers. There are street parties, games and lots of music and entertainment. The special food of Eed-ul-Fitr includes treats such as dates, baklava (a pastry drenched in honey and pistachio nuts), candies and cookies.

Closing Worship

Related Scripture Passages: Psalm 103, Luke 9:28-43
Prayer: Light a candle and say the following **Prayer of St. Columba of Iona** together.

        Be thou a bright flame before me
        Be thou a guiding star above me
        Be thou a smooth path below me
        Be thou a kindly shepherd behind me.
        Today, tonight, and forever. Amen.

Celebrations for Mardi Gras and Shrove Tuesday

Group Celebrations

- Head out to the local pancake restaurant for dinner on Tuesday night. Return to the church for a brief worship service, including the imposition of ashes (see **Shrove Tuesday or Ash Wednesday Service** in Section F).
- Have a costume party or dance! Make the atmosphere as festive as you like with balloons, streamers, a **Piñata** (see below), and refreshments like doughnuts or other sweets. Award prizes for costumes. Be sure to explain the traditions surrounding Shrove Tuesday.
- Make masks (see **Domino Masks** below or **Plaster Masks** on page 134). Encourage everyone to decorate their masks with symbols of their selves – the self others see and the parts of themselves they keep hidden. Talk about Lent as a time to remove our "masks" or false pretenses and be honest with ourselves, God, and others.

Domino Masks

You will need: lightweight cardboard (cereal boxes or large recipe cards will do), scissors or sharp art knife, hole punch, white glue, sequins, pipe cleaners, ribbon, inexpensive jewelry (e.g. rhinestones, plastic jewels), colored feathers, gummed stars, gold or silver spray paint, elastic (not bands, the kind you purchase in a fabric or craft store).

Instructions: Make a simple domino mask shape from lightweight cardboard. Hole punch the sides of the mask as shown and attach elastic to one side, stretching the elastic around your head so that it fits snugly, and attach it to the other side. Have group members help each other locate and trace where the eye-holes will be. Cut the eye-holes. Check to make sure these are positioned correctly and are large enough. Remove the mask for decorating. You may want to spray it with gold (silver) spray paint first. Then add details (sequins, gummed stars, feathers). Twist pipe cleaners around an eye-hole in a circular shape for an interesting effect.

Piñata

A piñata is a brightly decorated object (usually papier mâché) stuffed with candies, dried fruit, and other treats. These are seen at almost any type of celebration in Mexico and other parts of Latin America – at birthdays, Christmas, or anytime there is a *fiesta*!

You will need: round balloons, string, our, newspaper, water, tissue paper.

Instructions: Blow up the balloon and tie it. Wrap string around the balloon several times. Leave excess string at top. Tear 1 in. (2.5cm) strips of newspaper. Mix our and water to make a thin paste. Dip the strips in it and draw off the excess with your fingers. Place these strips over the balloon two or three layers thick, covering the string and balloon completely except for a circle about 1.5 in. (3.5cm) in diameter at the top of the balloon. When dry, paint or decorate. If you wish, cut 1 in. (2.5cm) squares of tissue paper. Place the eraser end of a pencil in the center of the square and twist the tissue around it. Dip this in glue and stick to papier mâché. Alternatively, at pieces of tissue paper can be glued on in overlapping layers.

Once it is decorated, pop the balloon and fill the hollow shell with candy, unshelled peanuts, etc. Tape the top shut. Suspend from the string at the top.

Congregational Celebrations

- Host a pancake dinner on Shrove Tuesday. (If you can't have a dinner on Tuesday evening, plan a pancake luncheon for the last Sunday before Lent.)
- Make special Shrove Tuesday placemats. Include some of the background information about the Season of Lent (see the introductory pages to this season). Add some graphics and leave spaces for kids to color. Place a cup of crayons on each table.
- Host a Mardi Gras costume celebration. This might include a pancake dinner or potluck, dance, Piñata (see the previous page), refreshments including doughnuts and other sweets, and of course – awards for costumes!
- Invite members of the congregation to come to the church Tuesday evening and bring ingredients like sugar, eggs, oil, milk, our, salt from home along with their favorite recipes. Bake bread, pie and other dishes that make use of these ingredients. You might sample some of your work and then donate the rest to a local soup kitchen or shelter.
- Plan a brief worship service after sundown on Tuesday evening to mark Ash Wednesday and help people move into the Season of Lent. During the service ask people to write something down on paper that they want forgiveness for or want to change about themselves. Burn these in a container along with the palm crosses or branches from the previous year's Palm Sunday (see **Shrove Tuesday or Ash Wednesday** Service in Section F).

Minimal Time Bread Recipe

Ingredients:

    1 pkg. yeast (1 level tablespoon [15ml])
    2 cups (500mL) warm water
    3 Tbsp. (45mL) sugar/honey
    2 tsp. (10mL) salt
    1/4 cup (60mL) oil
    7 cups (1.75L) our
    1 egg (for glaze)

Add the sugar to the warm water in a mixing bowl. Sprinkle the yeast into the warm sugar water. Let stand 5 minutes. Mix in salt, oil, and our a little at a time until you can work the dough with your hands. If sticky, add more our. Knead for 5 minutes. Form into a sculpture and brush with beaten raw egg. Let rise 10 min. Bake at 350⁰F (175⁰C) for 15-40 min. depending on size of figures. (Or make freeform loaves by shaping the dough into two rounds and placing them on a greased cookie sheet. Let rise and bake as above.)

Shrove Tuesday Fund Raising

- Host a pancake dinner on Shrove Tuesday. Make this a "pay-by-donation" event – either money or non-perishable goods for the local food bank.
- Sell or accept donations for providing treats like doughnuts with coffee on the Sunday before Lent. Explain the tradition of Mardi Gras to people so they'll understand why you're doing this. Use the money proceeds to support an outreach project or the overseas development fund of your denomination.

Pancake Recipe

Mix dry ingredients:

    1 1/2 cups (375mL) our
    3 Tbsp. (45mL) sugar
    1 3/4 teas. (8mL) baking powder
    1/2 tsp. (2mL) salt

In a separate bowl mix:

    1 1/4 cups (300mL) milk
    1 egg
    3 Tbsp. (45mL) oil

Combine with a whisk. Thin batter with water or milk as necessary.

Section D:

Mood and Flavor of the Season

The Season of Lent is 40 days (and six Sundays) long, stretching from Ash Wednesday to Holy Saturday. Our English word "Lent" comes from the word "lengthen." In the Northern Hemisphere, Lent takes place as the days lengthen into Spring. The liturgical color for Lent is purple, indicating a time of repentance. In Lent we take stock, both of ourselves and our society. We reflect on our efforts to implement the values of peace, community, and equality of all before God.

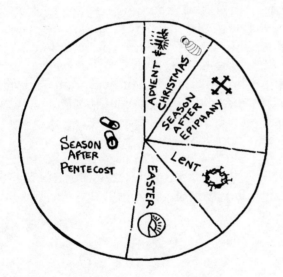

Special Days

Ash Wednesday marks the beginning of the Season of Lent. Some churches have a brief service either on Shrove Tuesday or early on Wednesday morning. It may include the ritual "imposition of ashes." Traditionally, the ashes that are placed on our foreheads in the sign of the cross are the ashes from the previous year's burning of Palm Sunday branches or palm crosses. This ritual reminds us of our own mortality and need for repentance, both as individuals and as communities. Ashes symbolize mourning and humility; when the Hebrews mourned, they put dust or ashes on their heads and wore sackcloth as signs of humility. The ashes placed on our foreheads on Ash Wednesday remind us of the many things in our world that are not as God wants.

Holy Week begins with Passion or Palm Sunday commemorating the triumphant entry of Jesus into Jerusalem. Semitic people have always regarded the palm tree as a tree of honor; in Jesus' day it marked the place where shepherds could find water for their flocks. Even today the branches of palm trees are placed on the graves of some Semitic people to symbolize eternal life.

Holy Week includes Maundy Thursday or Holy Thursday when we remember the Last Supper. People in many churches prepare together and celebrate a traditional Jewish seder meal on this evening. The term "Maundy" comes from the Latin "mandatum," which means "commandment." Scripture describes Jesus washing his disciples' feet at the Last Supper as a demonstration of how everyone – both servant and master – is to be treated equally (John 13:16). Then he commanded them to love one another (John 13:34). In English tradition, on this day the monarch distributes alms – food, clothing, and money – to the poor. As in early centuries, in some places today clergy symbolically wash the feet of parishioners on this day.

Holy Week culminates in Good Friday. Special worship services are held to remember Jesus' crucifixion. Why do we call such a painful day "good"? One suggestion is that "good" represents a vowel shift from an older form of "God's Friday." The change from God's Friday to Good Friday might parallel the one from "God be wi' ye" (God be with ye) to "good-bye." By calling this day "Good" Friday, we also acknowledge that God's love overcame the evil in the world that crucified Jesus, and transformed it into good for the whole world. The author of the Gospel of John affirmed this with these words: "The light shines in the darkness, and the darkness has never put it out" (John 1:5).

The Season of Lent ends on Holy Saturday, a day when many Christians keep an Easter vigil. This practice is often very popular with youth.

Our observances of Lent and its special days have evolved over the centuries. Christians in the first two centuries did not even commemorate Good Friday. They focused only on Easter Day. The first Christians met for worship on Holy Saturday around 6 p.m. They continued fasting, praying, and meditating through the night until about 3 a.m. on Easter Sunday. Then they celebrated the Eucharist. Many years later, fasting extended to include Friday. This period of 40 hours corresponds to the time Jesus' body lay in the tomb. Later still, the period of fasting extended to include all of Holy Week. By the year 600, the fast had extended to the 40 days (not including Sundays) prior to Easter. This time period reminds us of the 40 days Jesus spent in the wilderness preparing for public ministry. This became a time of final preparation for "catechumens" – those people who sought membership in the church by profession of faith and baptism. In time, many other church members undertook these 40 days of penitence and fasting for their own self-discipline. Reflecting on their own faith, these members joined with catechumens and renewed their baptismal promises at Easter.

Implications for Youth Ministry

The introspective mood of this season suggests many possible themes for Lenten programs. Lent provides a unique opportunity to slow down, to "look inside ourselves," and to reflect on our lives and our world. In the busy lives of many youth today, this can be a welcome invitation. So often they feel pressured by the world's preoccupation with outer appearances. Youth find it refreshing and affirming to take time examining "inner selves."

Lent can help us reestablish a balance between God, self, and others. The story of Jesus' life is full of themes for youth reflection – facing difficult decisions, temptations, fears about death, broken relationships. This may also be the time to discuss issues of faith and church membership with youth.

In many churches Lent is a time for fund raising for outreach projects, holding special gatherings, and preparing for the celebration of Easter. This may include planning special intergenerational services and events, preparing music and drama, or holding special study groups. These events provide opportunities for youth involvement in the life of the wider church community. With your clergy, try to plan ways that youth can organize, lead, and participate in the events of this season (see **Planning Special Events for Lent** on page 135).

Faith

Group Check-in

How do you define something like "faith"? It's hard to put into a few words (or into any words at all!) what our faith is and what it means to us. An analogy (a comparison) can sometimes help us. For example, consider the now famous saying that Tom Hanks uttered in the movie *Forrest Gump:* "Life is like a box of chocolates. You never know what you're goin' to get." Invite everyone to think about their own concept of "faith" and try to articulate it using an analogy. You might begin each phrase with "Faith is like..." (e.g. Faith is like falling off a cliff and knowing there's a bungy cord attached to you). Ask everyone to share and explain their analogy.

Household of Faith

Hand out copies of **Household of Faith** on pages 109-111. Ask four people to volunteer and tell the four stories. Afterwards discuss these questions as a group or in pairs:
• Which is your room or door? Explain how your faith journey has been similar.
• Do you know people who have entered through different doors? Which ones?

Faith Stories

People come to faith in Christ by differing paths and enter the church through different "doors." Similarly Jesus' followers came to faith in different ways. Divide into small groups and look up one of the passages listed below. Then create a short skit or pantomime to present this story to the others. After each, discuss how the person in the story found their faith.

> Acts 9:3-19 (Paul)
> John 3:1-13 (Nicodemus)
> Matthew 9:9-12 (Matthew)
> John 20:24-28 (Thomas)
> Luke 8:1-3 (Mary, Joanna, Susanna)
> John 1:43-51 (Philip and Nathanael)
> Acts 9:36 (Dorcas)
> Acts 10:1-4 (Cornelius)
> Acts 16:1 (Timothy)

Being Faithful

Ask everyone to rank the following two lists from 1-5 according to their importance (with 1 being the most important and 5 being the least important).
A) The most important action for a faithful person is
___ following the Ten Commandments
___ believing in God and Jesus Christ
___ following the teachings of the Bible
___ going to church
___ spending time in prayer and reflection
B) The most important action for a person faithful to Christ's teachings is
___ serving others
___ using the gifts and talents God has given them
___ loving their neighbor, caring for others
___ sharing their beliefs with others
___ being baptized or confirmed

Discuss with a partner the actions you ranked most important and least important in each list. Why did you rank them this way?

Faith Symbols

Gather an assortment of household items or pictures of them. Divide into small groups and give each one an item, newsprint, and a marker. Give the groups five minutes to record as many ideas as they can generate about how this item could be a symbol of faith. Your ideas can be as creative and outrageous as you like!

Faith Journey Map

We are all on our own faith journey. Each journey is different. Invite everyone to take a few minutes to reflect on their own faith journey: How has your faith developed? How did you come into the church? What have been some of the high points and some of the low points? Who has helped you? Where are you now in the journey? Hand out sheets of newsprint and markers and ask everyone to illustrate their personal faith journey by creating a road map. They may want to add words or drawings to symbolize the stops, starts, unexpected turns, and detours along the way.

Creating Faith Symbols

Read together **Faith Symbols of the Church** on page 126. Invite everyone to make their own symbol using these or something from their own experiences. Provide shrink art plastic, Fimo (a special craft plasticine that comes in many colors, but is expensive), clay or **Baker's Clay** (see page 159). Make sure you poke holes in these so they can be strung on leather thongs, or string, and worn. Fimo makes excellent jewelry like brooches, pins or pendants.
Variation: Decorate shoelaces with faith symbols. Permanent or washable markers will work though non-permanent designs will eventually wash out when the shoelaces are laundered.

Closing Worship

Related Scripture Passages: Colossians 2:6-7, Hebrews 11:1-3, John 11:17-27
Statement of Faith: Obtain a copy of a creed or statement of faith used in your denomination. Have a volunteer read it aloud. Then read together the following creed.

A Third World Creed

I believe that behind the mist the sun waits.
I believe that beyond the dark night it is raining stars.
I believe in secret volcanoes and the world below.
I believe that this lost ship will reach port.
They will not rob me of hope, it shall not be broken.
My voice is filled to over owing
with the desire to sing,
the desire to sing.
I believe in reason, and not in the force of arms;
I believe that peace will be sown throughout the earth.
I believe in our nobility, created in the image of God,
and with free will reaching for the skies.
They will not rob me of hope,
it shall not be broken,
it shall not be broken.

From *Confessing our Faith Around the World IV*, Chile , South America
(World Council of Churches 1985) Used by permission.

The Household of Faith

Our faith journeys are personal! Our faith is personal. It is a personal God to whom we relate. Our journeys will be as different as we are different as persons. We need to learn to affirm the journeys of others, particularly those that are radically different from ours. The gospel doesn't allow us to claim that our difference is the only way. Peter's experience was different from the experiences of Paul and Mary and Timothy and Thomas. The gospel does not know only one route into human lives.

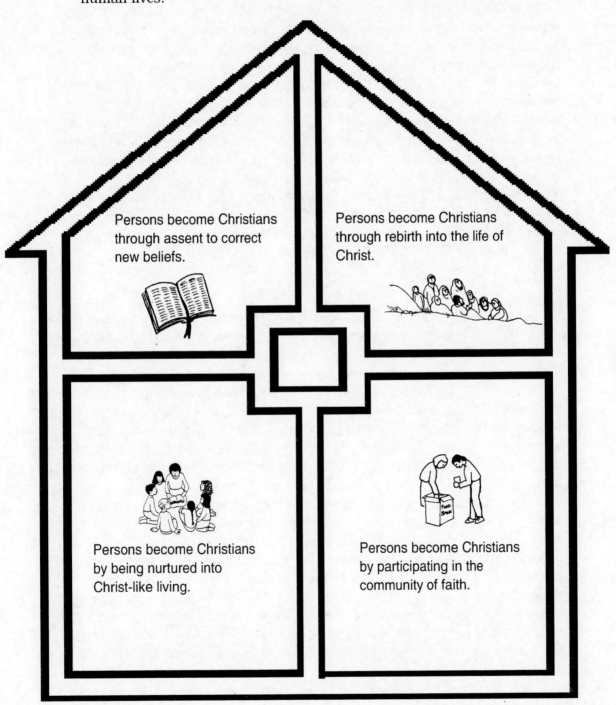

Persons become Christians through assent to correct new beliefs.

Persons become Christians through rebirth into the life of Christ.

Persons become Christians by being nurtured into Christ-like living.

Persons become Christians by participating in the community of faith.

Household of Faith Stories

Jack's Story

Jack is an ordinary Christian in many ways. He is like many believing people in our communities of faith. Jack is a school teacher, so perhaps it makes sense that, for Jack, intellectual validity is to be valued above everything else.

As a child Jack went to Sunday School regularly and belonged to Beavers and Scouts. He earned his Religion in Life badge at age 13.

Then came the confirmation class and it was reasonable to expect that he would "join" the church like everyone else, but he didn't. Surely he, a top student at high school, could understand what it was all about. And he did, mostly, but not all. There were some details that kept on bugging him – things like a virgin birth and physical resurrection. So Jack decided to "pass" on joining the church even though he still went regularly.

Then came university. To a "thinker" like Jack it was an exciting time. When he graduated with a degree in science he chose teaching as a career. He liked working with teenagers especially – they challenged him to continue his thinking about his own faith. They wouldn't let him off the hook. So he did more reading and searching. And then he had what he calls the great "aha!" of his faith. Things just made sense all of a sudden. He not only joined the church, he started teaching Sunday School.

Jack is still that ordinary kind of a Christian. Maybe he thinks a bit deeper about his faith than most. It has a deep personal meaning for his life. But Jack still needs to understand before he accepts anything as a part of his faith. Jack has come through the door of ASSENT TO CORRECT BELIEFS.

Carol's Story

Carol's pathway into the faith has been different. She's an exuberant person, loaded with personality, a fun person to be with. She's really involved in the life of her church and community. She's one of those people that makes you wonder what the church ever did without her.

She tells her story this way: "I was a happy teenager, had lots of friends. I didn't go to church. My parents weren't big on it. They said I could make up my own mind when I got older so they didn't mind that I sometimes went to church with my friend Jennie. She liked church and went a lot. We were both 16. One time a preacher came to a nearby city and Jennie invited me to go to hear him with her and her parents.

"What I was about to see and experience, I hadn't planned on. Not in my wildest dreams! This guy – his name was Billy Graham – was really something else. He really laid it on and I didn't feel too comfortable, you know. He talked about our 'separation from God' and 'sin' and 'heaven' – those kind of things. At the end he asked those who wanted to come forward to commit their lives to Jesus. I didn't move! I stayed right in my seat! But afterward, at home that night in bed, I couldn't stop thinking about everything he said. The next night Jennie's family went back and so I went with them – I felt a kind of 'tug.' And that night, at the end, I went forward. I wasn't forced. I did it voluntarily, with a sense of real commitment, and I asked Jesus to come into my life. And he did."

Carol is a mature 30-year-old. She bubbles with life, but she's not phony. She says she thinks it's important to be born again but she'd never push it on anyone because she believes that God reaches out to each of us in different ways. Carol entered the Household of Faith through the REBIRTH INTO THE NEW LIFE IN CHRIST door.

Household of Faith Stories

Jane's Story

Jane never went to church as a kid. Why would she? she asks. Her parents never went. Neither did any of her friends. You were kind of "out" if you were "in" to church in those days.

But Jane was "in" to everything else. If there was a cause to be involved with, Jane was there. Especially in university! She belonged to a human rights group, she wrote letters to people in government, she attended demonstrations and organized fund-raisers. When the issue was civil rights in El Salvador, Jane was in the thick of it. And then there was the Nestle Boycott! The issues Jane felt passionate about were justice, peace, human rights.

One night she dropped in on a rap session in her dorm. Some of her friends were there. They were Christians and the group was part of the SCM (Student Christian Movement). But that night they talked a language even Jane could understand. The words centered around "justice." She found some like-minded people in that group, that cared about the same things she did. There began the courtship of church and world for Jane. She started to attend church with some of the other students and she discovered that the world of street and pulpit weren't that far apart – that Jesus' call was a call to justice for all. So Jane came into the Household of Faith through THE COMMUNITY OF FAITH door.

Bob's Story

Bob feels like he's always been a part of the church. He can't really remember when he wasn't. It seems like he grew up in the church and can't remember a time when he wasn't a Christian. "I've always had a profound sense that God was with me so, for me, there didn't seem to be any reason to 'ask Jesus to come into my life.' He's already there."

When he was a kid his parents took him to church. They "took" him, didn't just "send" him, Bob points out. A lot of his friends used to hop on those buses – old school buses – and go to some churches across town that their parents didn't even know much about, much less attend. Bob's family "went as a family." Bob liked Sunday School. He was part of the choir and the youth group. He went to Church Camp every summer. And he was confirmed when he was 16. Later, as an adult, Bob found it quite natural to continue on to lead Adult Bible Study and take part in worship occasionally.

Bob doesn't remember ever being outside the church. Bob entered the church through the BEING NURTURED INTO CHRIST-LIKE LIVING door.

Adapted from *Being the Christian Story* by Gordon Bruce Turner, Division of Mission in Canada, © The United Church of Canada, Etobicoke, Canada. Reprinted by permission.

Choices

Group Check-in

Colors are often associated with feelings. Choose a color that describes how you're feeling right now. Explain your choices to each other.

Sorting Out Time

After Baptism in the Jordan and before beginning public ministry, Jesus went into the wilderness. The gospels describe how he fasted and prayed for 40 days and nights and was tempted by the devil. This was a time for Jesus to sort out what God was calling him to do and to be. He was faced with a lot of choices. During Lent, build time into your weekly gatherings to reflect on your own lives and the choices you are called to make. The following are some suggestions:

- Create **Wilderness Journals** (page 128) or try **Lenten Journaling** on page 124.
- Plan a fast and prayer vigil, perhaps for the Easter long weekend. See **40-Hour Fast** on page 116 and **Easter Vigil** on page 140 for ideas.
- Plan a Lenten retreat focusing on a theme like prayer, identity, self-esteem, or faith.
- Make **Sand Candles** for youth to use at home (see next page).

Simple Living

Some people put their faith into action during Lent by choosing to live more simply. They cut out desserts, avoid eating out, cut back on "extras," or eat simple food dishes. They donate the money they save to charity. What are some actions you could take to live more simply during Lent? Try one of the vegetarian recipes from this page at a Lenten retreat or vigil. Or you might want to experiment with cooking them at home.

Choices Scenario

Play the game **Choices Scenario**. See the instructions and cards on pages 114-115.

Simple Living Recipes

Malaysian Lentils and Rice (6 servings)
- 1 1/2 cups (375mL) lentils
- 3/4 can 10 oz (284 mL) condensed milk
- 1 can 10 oz (284 mL) mushroom soup
- 1 can 10 oz (284 mL) mushrooms
- 3 tsp. (15mL) curry
- 3 tsp. (15mL) turmeric
- 2 tsp. (10mL) salt
- 2 tsp. (10mL) chili powder

Cook lentils until tender. Drain. Add remaining ingredients and simmer. Cook rice separately. *To serve:* Ladle a generous amount of mixture over rice and garnish with coconut, tidbits of pineapple and bananas, raisins, unsalted peanuts, and diced cucumber.

Vegetarian Chili and Tacos (6-8 servings)
- 3 cups (750mL) dry kidney beans
- 9 (2.3L) cups water
- 2 tsp. (10mL) salt
- 14 oz tin (398 mL) of tomato sauce
- 1 cup (250 mL) raw bulgar wheat
- 2 tsp. (10 mL) vegetable oil
- 3 cloves garlic
- 1 1/2 cups (375 mL) chopped onion
- 2 celery stalks, chopped
- 1 green bell pepper, chopped
- 28 oz. (875g) can stewed tomatoes
- 1 1/2 tsp. (7mL) chili powder
- 1 tsp. (5mL) cumin seed
- 1 tsp. (5mL) salt
- 1/2 tsp. (2mL) black pepper
- dash cayenne
- 1/2 tsp. (2mL) dried basil
- 14 oz (420g) can mushrooms
- 1 cup (250mL) diced low fat cheese
- 1/4 cup (60mL) chopped parsley

Soak beans overnight to soften. Drain. Add water and 2 tsp. (10mL) salt to beans. Cook covered

(continued on next page)

until tender, about 2 hours. Drain. Heat tomato sauce to boil in large saucepan. Add raw bulgar and cover; let stand at least 15 min. Heat vegetable oil in skillet and sauté garlic and onion. Add celery and green pepper. Cook 5 min. Add to bulgar pot all ingredients including the drained beans. Cover and cook over medium heat until tender, about 1 1/2 hours.

To serve as tacos: Provide tortilla chips and garnish – chopped lettuce, tomato, cucumber, grated cheddar, sour cream, black olives and salsa. *Buen provecho!*

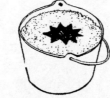

1. Place sand in pail.   2. Prepare shape in sand.

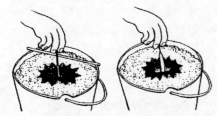

3a. Add wicking. OR 3b. Add old candle.

4. Pour wax.

Sand Candles

You will need: wax (purchase paraffin wax or melt down old candles), wicking (purchase from a craft store, use old candle wicks left from melting down used candles, or use an actual candle and add more wax around it), sticks and weights (if using wicking you will need a stick and weights to hold wicking firmly in place – chopsticks work well), 48-oz. (1.5 L) can to hold wax and saucepan of water to set it in (or an old double boiler), colored crayons, damp sand, oven mitts.

Instructions: Pack damp sand into a box or bucket. Hollow out an interesting shape in the sand for your candle. These shapes can be created with your hands, bottle, pencils, sticks – anything that can be pressed into the sand to make a hollow.

Place a wick into the center of the mold by tying one end to a stick suspended across the top of the mold. On the other end, tie a weight and drop into the hollow so the wick hangs straight down and is taut. (Or suspend a candle by its wick into the hollow and pour hot wax around.)

Melt wax in the top of a double boiler (or in a can placed in a saucepan of boiling water). **Warning: Wax reaches a flash point at approx. 200°C/400°F. It should never get this hot.** Add colored crayons to the melted wax to give it interesting colors if you wish. Using oven mitts to hold the pot, pour melted wax into moist sand mold. Different colored wax poured in layers makes interesting effects. Leave wax in sand until completely hard. Then remove candle and wash off excess sand.

(***Note:*** If you live near a beach, create these candles in the sand there. Combine this activity with a hot-dog or marshmallow roast and a worship!)

Closing Worship

Related Scripture Passages: Deuteronomy 30:15-20, Matthew 4:1-11
Sing: Sing together the simple song found on page 165 of Resource Section F. Try it as a round.

Choices Scenario

Instructions: Photocopy this page and the **Answer Cards** on page 96. Mount on cardboard backing if you wish, and cut apart. This game is like Scruples™. The object is to get rid of your **Choices Scenario** cards. Deal each player one answer card face down. Deal out two or more Choices Scenario cards (depending on the size of your group) to each player. Moving clockwise from the dealer, the first player chooses one of their scenario questions to ask any other player. Ask someone you think will respond with the same answer as the answer card you have in your hand. If you get the answer you were looking for, you may discard the scenario card. No matter how the person responds, discard your answer card and select a new one each turn.

✂ *cut apart on lines*

Your parents have forbidden you to go to a party because there will likely be alcohol. They go out for the evening and your friend calls, urging you to go because "what your parents don't know won't hurt them." Do you go to the party?

You overhear some kids at school talking about a prank they pulled. Some property was destroyed. That evening you hear about it on TV and the police ask for information about the crime. Do you phone the anonymous tips line?

You arrive at the theater to find a long line of people waiting for tickets. You see someone you know near the front of the line. Do you ask to be let into the line with them?

A friend shoplifts a pair of jeans without you noticing. After you've left the shop your friend shows you the jeans and asks you to carry them in your backpack. Do you?

A car runs over a cat. You see the driver and know the person, who goes to your church. Do you tell the cat's owner who the driver was?

Your older sibling has a party when your parents aren't home. Your parents suspect the truth and ask you if anything happened while they were away. Do you tell them?

One evening you suddenly remember about a test at school the next day. You aren't prepared. Do you pretend to be sick the next day?

After arriving home from a friend's house you discover you accidentally brought something of theirs home with you. It doesn't look important and may not be missed. Do you tell them?

A good friend has just bought a new sweater and asks if you like it. You think it's awful. Do you say so?

During a test you hear two other students discussing the answer to a test question. The teacher doesn't hear them. It's question you haven't been able to answer. Do you write down the answer you overheard?

Choices Scenario

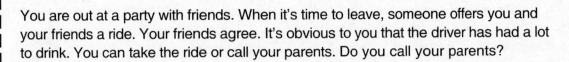

You are out at a party with friends. When it's time to leave, someone offers you and your friends a ride. Your friends agree. It's obvious to you that the driver has had a lot to drink. You can take the ride or call your parents. Do you call your parents?

Some friends surprise you with a cake they baked for your birthday but it's a kind you just hate. Do you tell them?

Friends in your group have been talking about someone that you know and like. You know what they are saying is mean and untrue. Do you defend the other person?

You promise to visit a friend who is sick, but then get invited to go away for the day with another friend. Do you go away anyway?

You are riding your bike and pass a parked car too closely. Your pedal scrapes paint off the car. Do you keep on riding away?

Your parents lend you the car to drive to a friend's house. When you get there your friend suggests you drive downtown to the movies. Do you call your parents to get permission?

You find a twenty dollar bill on the ground. Do you try to find out whom it belongs to?

Your parents ask you if you have ever experimented with alcohol. You have. Do you tell them the truth?

On an exam just handed back to you, you notice that an adding mistake has made your mark higher than it should be. Do you tell your teacher?

You and two others complete a school project at school. You get an excellent grade but one person does very little work. Do you bring this up with the teacher?

40-Hour Fast

(A fast from 8 p.m. Friday to 12 noon Sunday is 40 hours.
Make your fast whatever length is appropriate for your group.)

Set the Date

Set the date for the weekend event starting as early as Friday evening or Saturday afternoon but to end at the close of the worship service Sunday morning. A weekend fast will not be harmful to an adolescent if the fast is one that allows for appropriate rest and the drinking of water.

Prepare Sponsor and Information Sheets

Prepare sponsor sheets for collecting the names, addresses, phone numbers and signatures of persons pledging to pay a certain amount of money for each hour the youth fasts. Give some to each participant. Prepare information sheets for participants' parents or guardians to sign, indicating that they understand the program, that there will be fasting, and that they give permission for their youth to participate. On a six-hour basis, have a leader sign a Fasting Form like the one below indicating the number of hours of fasting completed.

Recommendation

A special drink is recommended for fasting to keep stomachs from growling.

Recipe

Lemon juice, water, pure maple syrup to sweeten (must be pure maple syrup), dash of cayenne.(The cayenne helps keep the body temperature up and blood circulating.)

Fasting Form

has completed

6 hours without food

_____
                        leader's signature

12 hours without food

_____
                        leader's signature

18 hours without food

_____
                        leader's signature

for a final total of _____ hours.

Other Suggestions

- Do lots of advertising ahead of time about what the group is doing and what the money it raises is going to support.

- Light a candle as you begin your fast as a symbol of the road you are journeying on behalf of the world's hungry. Extinguish it at the end of the fast.

- Set the tone for the fast with an opening worship. Acknowledge that this is an important time for identifying with those in our world who are experiencing hunger and malnutrition.

- It is important that the youth agree to use the sleeping hours for sleep.

- Bring a variety of board games and plan active games such as volleyball.

- Plan to do some crafts together.

- Bring Bibles and Concordances. Have the youth learn about fasting in biblical days, and talk about why fasting is considered a spiritual act.

- Arrange to show films that help explore the causes of hunger in our world.

- Make posters and banners, and write prayers to share with the congregation on Sunday morning.

- Learn songs about the needs of the "Two-Thirds World."

- Invite a guest speaker to join your group for part of the program – someone who has first-hand experience with poverty and hunger in our own country or in the world situation.

- Invite the minister(s) to join you for a special time of re ection and prayers Saturday evening before you sleep.

Prayer

Group Check-in

Create a list of three things and ask everyone to choose which they feel most like (e.g. a drop of water, calm lake, stormy ocean). Explain to each other why you are feeling that way today.

Forms of Prayer

Experience one or more of these different forms of prayer together as a group.

- Read the **Body Movement Prayer** and do the motions (see page 119). This prayer incorporates simple movements based on Tai Chi. Try doing this out-of-doors or as a morning worship in a retreat setting. Begin with some stretching exercises.
- Read the litany prayer **Teach Us and Show Us God's Way** on page 157. This was written by a youth group. Try to read this together outside or with photographs or posters of nature displayed in your room.
- Listen to some Taizé musical pieces if you can obtain these. Teach one or two of these to the group. The words are often in Latin. Many of these pieces have come from the church in the Middle Ages and were used by monks for meditation purposes. What music today is suitable for times of prayer and meditation? Encourage group members to share their ideas with each other.

Pretzel Making

Since the early days of the Christian Church, Lent has been a season of serious self-examination, prayer, and fasting. It marks the 40 days Jesus spent in the desert praying and fasting in preparation for his public ministry. In the fifth century, monks began the tradition of baking and distributing pretzels on certain days before Easter. The dough, twisted in the shape of two arms crossed in prayer, were symbols reminding people of their need for repentance. In several European countries today including Germany and Austria, pretzels are hung from palm branches on Palm Sunday. Make pretzels using the recipe on this page.

Pretzels

1 1/3 cups (325mL) warm water
1 Tbsp. (15mL) sugar
1 Tbsp. (15mL) yeast (or one package)
1 tsp. (5mL) salt
3 1/2 cups (875mL) our
coarse salt
1 1/2 Tbsp. (22mL) milk
1 egg yolk

Put 1/2 cup (125mL) warm water in a warmed medium-sized mixing bowl and stir in sugar. Sprinkle yeast on top and leave for 10 min. Add remaining water and salt and stir. Add our, stirring in 2 1/2 cups (625mL) with spoon then kneading in the last cup with hands. Turn onto a oured surface and knead until smooth. Can be shaped right away.

To shape pretzels: Take a piece of dough the size of a walnut and roll into a long "snake." Bend two ends around and cross over. Pinch dough together where it touches. Mix egg yolk and milk together and brush over each pretzel. Sprinkle with coarse salt. Bake at 400ºF (200ºC) for about 15 min. or until brown.

(**Alternative:** Use refrigerated bread stick dough to form pretzels. Shape and brush with egg yolk and milk mixture. Bake according to package directions.)

Prayer Tree

Make a prayer tree for your church. Invite members of the congregation to write prayer concerns on slips of paper attached to pretzels and hang these on a tree (a bare branch set in sand or plaster of Paris). The group might take responsibility for incorporating these into the prayers of the people for the weeks of Lent.

Prayer Knot Necklace

Make a series of 40 knots approx. 1/2 in. (1cm) apart in an 18 in. (45cm) length of leather thong or thin black cord (as used to make necklaces with pendants). Each knot represents 1 day in Lent, beginning on Ash Wednesday and lasting 40 days (excluding Sundays). Encourage the youth to wear these as reminders of the self-reflective and penitent mood of Lent, and as a reminder to pray. Try using the following discipline for praying the Ten Commandments:

1. Help me to keep God at the center of my life.
2. Help me to think first of what God wants when I make choices.
3. Help me to reflect my love of God in what I say and do.
4. Help me to keep Sunday as a special day of worship and rest.
5. Help me to listen to and respect those who care for me.
6. Help me to care for all living things and to be a peacemaker.
7. Help me to care for my body and respect others.
8. Help me to not take anything that is not mine.
9. Help me to be truthful and fair to everyone.
10. Help me to be faithful to those I love.

Lenten Meditations

Many people choose to take on the discipline of daily prayer during Lent. Sometimes when we pray or meditate it helps to focus on a word or image. Give everyone small paper bags (like the ones you get in a candy store) and a set of **Lenten Meditations** (see page 121). These cards can be placed in the bag (or in a container) and one drawn each day throughout Lent. Encourage everyone to think about the significance of the words on the cards for them for that day or week and focus on this in their prayer and meditation.

Prayers for God's People

Obtain the book *With All God's People – The New Ecumenical Prayer Cycle*, compiled by John Carden, World Council of Churches, Geneva, 1990. In this book certain countries are lifted up in prayer each week of the year. Read some of the prayers together. Then invite everyone to write a prayer lifting up a group of God's people that concern them – a group in your community, your country, or in another part of the world. Work individually or in pairs. Refer to **Praying with Youth** on page 122 for ideas about different types of prayers.

Closing Worship

Related Scripture Passages: Matthew 6:5-13, Ephesians 6:18, Philippians 4:6-7

Meditation: We often focus on the stories of Jesus' active ministry – his healing, preaching, and teaching with the crowds and his disciples. However, we often overlook the fact that Jesus spent a lot of time in prayer. Invite everyone to find a space away from others, where they will not be distracted. Explain this process: You will read some Bible passages that describe Jesus praying. They may wish to close their eyes to listen. You will pause after each one and ask a question. There will be some time for silent prayer and reflection before you read the next passage.

Luke 6:12-13	What difficult choices are you faced with?
Mark 1:35-39	What are the distractions that keep you from taking time to pray?
Matthew 14:22-23a	How does prayer make you feel?
Luke 9:28-29	What transforming effect does prayer have on you?
John 17:1, 6-8, 11	What concerns do you have for your friends and family?
Luke 22:39-46	What are you struggling with that you could ask God's help with?
Mark 15:33-34	When have you felt abandoned by God and when have you felt God's presence in your life?

Prayer: Repeat together The Lord's Prayer.

Body Movement Prayer

(Based very loosely on traditional Tai Chi movements)

Stand with feet flat on the floor, shoulder-width apart, knees loose – slightly bent. All movements are done extremely slowly and consciously, with gestures flowing into one another with the same rhythm throughout, with arms returning to the Chi (center – just above the navel) after each movement. Begin by taking some deep breaths in through your mouth.

Movement #1: *Bring your arms up, and move them outwards with a very slow movement like opening curtains. Return to the Chi position.*

Prayer: Here, God, are my eyes. These are the eyes that fill with tears in sadness; that wrinkle in laughter. These are the eyes that are marked by laugh lines and worry lines. These are the eyes I see things with: things all around us – things that are breathtaking and beautiful. And things that need changing. Here, God, are my eyes.
Repeat movement #1 described above.

Prayer: Here, God, are my ears. These are the ears that don't always hear everything that's said. These are ears that love music; have overheard arguments late at night; have listened for hours to others' pain; ears that heard my mother's voice even before I was born; ears that have heard "I love you." Here, God, are my ears.
Repeat movement #1 described above.

Prayer: Here, God, are my vocal cords. These are the vocal cords that ache when I'm trying to talk without crying, or be heard when no one is listening. These are vocal cords that have shrieked with laughter – and pain; hummed in the silence; whispered into the dark late at night; raised in protest and in song. Here, God, are my vocal cords.
Repeat movement #1 described above.

Movement #2: *Bend both arms at the elbow. Bend both knees, making sure that they are at least shoulder-width apart. Lower yourself a few inches as if moving into a squatting position (see illustration). Bring your palms together in front of you. Keeping palms together, slowly raise your arms upward. Then let your palms open, keeping them joined at the heel of the hand or wrist (as if they were tied).*

Prayer: Here, God, are my hands. These are the hands I give and receive with. These are the hands I work with. These are the hands I serve with. These are the hundreds of nerve endings I touch and feel with. These are hands that have held others' hands, held babies, held caterpillars, held sand. Here, God, are my hands.
Bring hands back to the Chi position. Repeat movement #2 described above.

Movement #3: *Bring your arms down to the Chi position (just above the navel). Cross your wrists so that your palms are facing up. Extend your arms (with wrists crossed) out from your body a comfortable distance – your elbows should be slightly bent).*

(continued on next page)

Prayer: Here, God, is my blood. This blood that moves through my veins and my arteries. The blood that is the drumbeat in my ears when I am anxious or frightened; when I'm first in love; when the other parts of me are moving. Here, God, is my blood.
Repeat movement #3 described above.

Movement #4: *Draw arms around in a wide circular motion, bringing your hands (cupped) into your heart.*

Prayer: Here, God, is the heart that pumps the blood that keeps me alive. This is the heart that sometimes feels too small, sometimes feels too big. This is the heart that aches sometimes – filling and emptying over and over like my life – filling and emptying of joy and pain. Here, God, is my heart.
Then draw arms outward again, from the heart, in a wide circular motion, returning to the Chi.

Movement #5: *Reach around to the right with your arm extended (a small scooping motion) as if you were gathering something in to the Chi. Repeat the action using the left arm. Both hands should end up at the Chi, cupped and palms facing upward. Your elbows should be slightly bent.*

Prayer: Here, God, are my insides. All the things that work and don't work. Parts of me I may never see but parts of me I know are there. Here, God, are my insides.
Repeat movement #5 described above.

Movement #6: *Reach up to the right – taking a short step to the right (heel first when placing your foot down). Raising your right arm and stepping at the same time helps you keep your balance.*

Prayer: Here, God, are my feet. These are the feet that carry me from place to place, willingly or unwillingly. These are feet that have been in many places, that jog and wear comfortable shoes, and stand in line a lot, and dance. These are feet that have raced across hot pavement, gotten slivers and grown out of shoes. Here, God, are my feet.
Return to Chi position. Repeat the motion with the left arm raised – taking a short step to the left (placing the heel down first as you place the foot down). Return to Chi position.

Movement #7: *Stretch your whole being wide open (arms raised and apart above your head) and then slowly lower them back to the Chi position. Breathe deeply in and out.*

Prayer: Here, God, are our whole bodies – originals, not copies – masterpieces you created in your own image.
We open our **eyes** to see beauty,
ears to hear harmony,
mouths and **throats** to utter truth,
hearts to give our love.
May we continue, this day, to worship you with our whole selves – in our working and resting, praying and being. Amen.

Lenten Meditations

Cut apart on lines. Hand out sets of Lenten Meditations with the instructions.

Instructions: Keep these Lenten Meditations in a bag or container. Draw one out each day of Lent. What images and feelings does that word bring to you? How does the word relate to your life? Spend a few minutes praying, thinking, drawing, or writing about the word.

peace	power	perseverance	strength	action	re ection	decision	guidance
faith	God	community	criticism	prayer	concern	value	discipleship
gratitude	compassion	direction	joy	friendship	enthusiasm	responsibility	resurrection
inspiration	simplicity	education	healing	patience	creativity	light	tenderness
truth	grace	love	abundance	openness	courage	integrity	sadness
clarity	understanding	communication	obedience	balance	expectancy	freedom	forgiveness
exibility	transformation	trust	spontaneity	purification	willingness	harmony	purpose

Praying with Youth

People pray in many different ways so there are many different types of prayers.
Here are some ideas for youth on creating and using a variety of prayers.

Squeeze Prayers

Form a circle, holding hands. The first person says a short sentence prayer, then squeezes the hand of the person to their left. That person says a prayer (aloud or silently), then squeezes the hand of the next person, and so on. When the squeeze returns to the first person, they say "Amen" and everyone responds "Amen." This works well with prayers of thanksgiving and of intercession. Make sure participants have the choice of saying their prayers silently or aloud. Some people are uncomfortable praying out loud in a group.

Litany Prayers

In a litany prayer, a leader reads one or two lines at a time, then the group repeats a responsive phrase. In a prayer of thanksgiving, for instance, the response could be, "We praise you, O God." In a prayer of intercession the response might be "O God, hear our prayer." Try it by brainstorming concerns of group members. Decide on a responsive phrase. Then divide the prayer into sections, indicating where the response will come. Alternatively, individuals or pairs could write sections of a prayer, ending with a predetermined phrase, like "O God, hear our prayer," to which the whole group responds, "And in your love, answer." See the examples of litany prayers on pages 61 and 157.

Add-On Prayers

Begin with a simple sentence and invite people to add phrases or a single word to complete the sentence (e.g. "God, we are concerned about..." or "Thank you God for..."). Allow silent time for people to pray. End the prayer with a phrase like "In Jesus' name" or "We know you are with us always" and then "Amen."

Responsive Prayers

Responsive prayers are similar to litanies. The leader or one group of people reads several lines. Then other group members read a response that is usually different every time. We often read sections of the Book of Psalms in this way. Try it by dividing the group in two and read alternating lines of a psalm. This is also called reading "antiphonally." See the examples of responsive prayers on pages 122 and 141.

Visual Prayers

We can pray silently through visual art. Sometimes these prayers need a few words to begin (e.g. "Loving God, through this art we express our concerns to you") and a closing phrase ("O God, hear the concerns of our hearts and minds. Amen"). Try a collage prayer (page 34) or slide prayer (page 40). Often these have a strong emotional impact on participants.

Creating a prayer by clustering

Write a word in the center of a piece of paper. All around it, put down ideas associated with it. What does it make you think about? What are other similar or related words? Write down all of your ideas. When you've filled the page, look over the words. Do they reveal anything? Do they spark other ideas? Try writing a prayer using some or all of the words you have written.

Writing a psalm for today

The psalms are a collection of prayers and songs. Jim Taylor, in his book *Everyday Psalms: The power of the Psalms in language and images for today*, attempted to present the psalms as the original psalmists might have written them, if they were living in our time. Choose a prayer from the Book of Psalms and use these suggestions from Jim to write your own prayer:

- Identify the main feeling of the psalm (e.g. anger, loneliness, joy, frustration).
- Think of a situation in which you've had that same feeling.
- Paraphrase the psalm around that situation following the structure of the verses of the psalm. When the psalm shifts (e.g. from lament to praise, from uncertainty to confidence) so should you.

Read your paraphrased psalm aloud and make any changes needed to make it ow poetically.

Idea Page #4 — Death and Grieving

Group Check-in

Invite everyone to describe how they are feeling in the form of a weather report (e.g. cloudy with some showers, but the forecast is for sun). Explain to each other why you are feeling that way.

Symbols of Death and Grieving

Set out some items like a funeral service bulletin, bare branch, nail, sympathy card, stuffed animal, piece of black fabric, and picture of a tombstone. Ask everyone to choose one that represents death and grieving to them. Share with a partner why you chose that symbol.

In the large group, talk about your experiences of death. What happens at a funeral? What do you know about burial and cremation? Do different cultures and religions have different ways of dealing with death? What happens to people after they die? Encourage everyone to ask questions and to share their experiences and beliefs about death. If there are many unanswered questions, the group might decide to explore this subject further by doing some research.

Feelings about Death

There are books written to help children deal with death and their feelings of grief (see box below). Bring one of these books. Pass it around with everyone reading a page. What do you think about the ideas expressed in the book? Would the book comfort a child? How?

Children's Books about Death

The Tenth Good Thing About Barney. Judith Viorst. New York: Alladin Books, 1988.

Freddy the Leaf. Leo Buscaglia. Toronto: Holt, Rinehart and Winston, 1982.

Badger's Parting Gift. Susan Varley. New York: William Morrow & Company, Inc., 1994.

Remember the Secret. Elisabeth Kubler-Ross. Berkley: Celestial Arts, 1982.

The Sky Goes on Forever. Molly MacGregor. Clearlake, Calif.: Dawn Horse Press, 1989.

Waterbugs and Dragonflies: Explaining Death to Young Children. Doris Stickney. New York: Pilgrim Press, 1982.

Plan this program well in advance and inform youth and parents about it. Consult with parents and clergy to identify youth who have experienced a recent loss or are currently faced with the death of someone close to them. This will help you understand the feelings and questions that might arise. A program about death and grieving, and the associated fears and beliefs, may arouse difficult, emotional memories. It may also provide a very valuable opportunity for youth to talk about a subject that is often on their minds.

Stories about Life and Death

Here are some Bible stories about death and life after death:

Matthew 22:23-33	Matthew 27:3-10
Mark 5:21-24, 35-42	Luke 7:11-17
John 11:38-44	1 Kings 17:17-23

Divide into small groups with each looking up a different story. After reading the passage, think up about five "I wonder...?" questions (e.g. "I wonder how the disciples felt when Judas hanged himself...?"). Record questions on a sheet of newsprint. Then share a paraphrase of the story and these wonder questions with the whole group.

In asking "I wonder...?" questions, the participants have laid the groundwork for a discussion about their own questions and beliefs about life and life after death. For example, after reading the story of Judas' death, someone may wonder about God's view of suicide. This may spark an important conversation on this subject.

Funeral Home Visit

Plan a tour of a funeral home (and include sufficient time afterwards to debrief). Consult your clergy for the name of a funeral home used frequently by members of your church. Call ahead to inquire about taking the youth on a tour and talking with employees about the role of undertaker. Go over what the tour will include so you know what the youth will experience.

Funeral directors or undertakers often play an important pastoral role in helping people come to terms with death and begin grieving. Many are particularly concerned about how young people are involved in the funeral preparations, and how this can affect their process of grief and dealing with loss. They have experience in talking openly and frankly about death. There are very few questions anyone could ask that would shock them. If group members feel inhibited, suggest they write their questions on paper. Read them out anonymously for the undertaker to answer.

Funeral Home Follow-up

If your group toured a funeral home, plan meeting time to share feelings and impressions about the experience. Accept all the feelings people express (e.g. "Kinda creepy" could refer to awe, mystery, surprise, or discomfort). Make a card for the undertaker, signed by all participants with some of the adjectives describing reactions to the experience. Would the group like to follow up further by having a discussion, seeing a film, or reading a book on the subject of life after death (e.g. *The Last Battle* by C.S. Lewis)?

For many of us the term "undertaker" conjures up pictures of graven-faced men in black and top hats measuring living people for the caskets they will eventually need. The origin of the term is to "undertake" funeral arrangements on behalf of the family. Many undertakers today prefer this title to "funeral directors" because that term can imply one who directs and takes control of a funeral, without considering the family's needs or resources.

Lenten Journaling

The Season of Lent is a time of introspection. Journal writing is an excellent way to encourage reflection on experiences. Make journals and invite everyone to write some of their thoughts and feelings in these. Buy inexpensive notebooks or duotang folders and loose-leaf paper to create the journals. The covers can be decorated with magazine pictures, words, or drawings that represent something about themselves.

Normally no one but the owner sees the journal. However, one youth leader suggested group members write in their journals any questions or suggestions of things they'd like to discuss. With their permission, this youth leader read what the youth wrote and wrote a response in the journal. These journals became a way for the leader and youth to communicate confidentially. The leader welcomed this opportunity to learn more about the concerns and interests of the group members.

Closing Worship

Related Scripture Passages: Psalm 23, 1 Corinthians 15:42-44, Revelation 21:1-4

Meditation: Ask group members to think about someone who has died whom they wish to remember. This could be someone close to them. (Or they might wish to focus on Jesus.) Ask them to try to picture that person in their minds. Read aloud to them **Death Is Nothing at All** on the next page. Silently meditate for a few minutes. Then ask these questions: How did you feel when you heard this reading? Was it comforting? What do you believe happens to someone after they've died?

Death Is Nothing at All

Death is nothing at all. It does not count. I have only slipped away into the next room. Nothing has happened. Everything remains exactly as it was. I am I, you are you, and the old life that we lived so fondly together is untouched, unchanged. Whatever we were to each other, that we are still. Call me by the old familiar name. Speak of me in the easy way which you always used. Put no difference in your tone. Wear no forced air of solemnity or sorrow. Laugh as we always laughed at the little jokes that we enjoyed together. Play, smile, think of me, pray for me. Let my name be ever the household word that it always was. Let it be spoken without an effort, without the ghost of a shadow upon it. Life means all that it ever meant. It is the same as it ever was. There is absolute and unbroken continuity...I am but waiting for you, for an interval, somewhere very near, just round the corner.

All is well.

Henry Scott Holland, 1847-1918, Canon of St. Paul's Cathedral.

Faith Symbols of the Church

Many of the faith symbols of the Christian Church are things that were part of the everyday lives of people in Jesus' day. These took on special significance because of something Jesus said or an association people made with them.

For instance, the water jug and basin symbolize service and caring for others because Jesus washed the disciples' feet at the Last Supper. Salt is a symbol of strength and perseverance because it was important for protecting food from decay and giving it flavor. Jesus used salt as an analogy for the faithful: "You are like salt for all humankind. But if salt loses its saltiness, there is no way to make it salty again." (Matthew 5:13) Jesus often used common, everyday experiences to illustrate his teachings.

 The fish is a symbol for followers of Christ because the five Greek letters forming the word "fish" are the first letters of the five words: Jesus Christ, Son of God, Savior.

 The rainbow is a symbol of reconciliation and hope because it appeared after the Flood.

 Since olive trees provide shelter and opportunity for rest, and olive oil is used for ointments, the olive branch is a symbol of peace, harmony and healing.

 Butterflies are symbols of resurrection, new life and new beginnings.

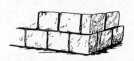 Rocks are a symbol for God and faith. This meaning comes from the story of water bursting forth when Moses struck the rock in the desert. Peter's faith is referred to as a rock, the foundation on which Christ would build his Church.

 A lamp is a symbol for the Scriptures, probably originating with "Thy word is a lamp unto my feet." (Psalm 119:105)

 The pearl is a symbol of faith and salvation. Jesus used it to describe the Kingdom of Heaven in a parable. (Matthew 13:45)

 A dove with an olive sprig is sometimes used as a symbol for the Flood. It denotes peace, forgiveness, and anticipation of new life.

Idea Page #5 Difficult Times, Suicide

Group Check-in

Ask everyone to think over the past week and remember a strong feeling they had. Then have them choose a sound (one that exists or one they've made up themselves) that represents that feeling (e.g. Groan! Shhhh! Argh!). On the count of three, ask everyone to make their sound. Do this more than once so that everyone can make their sound while also paying attention to the sounds others are making.

Poems of Difficult Times

Read the two poems **I'm Sitting in the Dark** and **You Will Never Know** on this page. People in their mid-teens wrote both of these poems. What feelings are expressed in these poems? Which of these authors do you think is at risk of suicide? Why do you think so? What puts them at risk?

In fact both authors may be at risk. Anyone who has suffered a loss, like the death of someone they love, can be at risk. The grief and sadness that Elisabeth feels can put a person at risk. So can the feelings of extreme hopelessness that Peter expresses in his poem.

Difficult Situations

What can cause someone to feel suicidal? Brainstorm a list as a group. Then divide into small groups and ask each to pick one situation to discuss. What might be some "warning signs" that someone having had this sort of experience is feeling suicidal? How do others react to these signs? How can others help a person with these feelings? Invite groups to plan and present a drama of their situation. Afterwards, discuss the "warning signs" they saw in the dramas. What help did people feeling suicidal receive? For resource information, see **Adolescent Suicide** on page 130.

I'm Sitting in the Dark

I'm sitting in the dark, there is no light
Sitting in darkness in a box which
I am locked inside and there is nothing
Inside this box, I stumble in the dark
And I search for something which I can't find
And there is no way out of this box. And I
Search and search and search and
I don't even know
What I'm looking for, and I'll probably die
In that nothing box, searching for nothing.

by Peter
From *Growing up Dead* by Brenda Rabkin, published by
McClelland and Stewart Limited, 1978.
Used by permission.

You Will Never Know

You will never know
How much I loved being your big sister
How I would lie in bed at night
And wait until you were home.

You will never know
How I would pretend to be asleep
As I heard you say goodnight to Fudge
And quietly pass by my door.

You will never know
How on the last night you left the house
I waited wide awake listening for your
familiar sound
But that sound never happened and
you never
Passed by my door.

The house is so quiet now and the only sound
Is from myself – crying.
Because you will never know how much I miss
Being your big sister.

by Elisabeth Cannon
From the *National Newsletter of the Compassionate Friend*

Lossip Theater

Think of a situation where someone is at risk of suicide. Use the Lossip Theater process from the Caribbean to reflect on it. This process is especially suitable for large groups.

Process: Ask some group members to dramatize the situation. Ask the "audience" to intervene in the action and make suggestions. Or they can enter the scene to take the place of someone in the scene or as an additional character. Respond as people might in the real life situation. Stop the action by clapping loudly or shouting "freeze!" The audience member is then free to enter the scene themselves or suggest a change to one of the other characters. The drama continues to a logical point of ending. Encourage everyone to talk about what they saw and how they felt. What different possibilities were identified for dealing with the issue? What are some other possibilities?

Wilderness Journaling

For the Hebrew people, the "wilderness" was a place of danger – full of wild animals, thieves, poisonous snakes – and a place of quiet and solitude. For Jesus, who often spent time alone in the wilderness or desert, it was both a place of escape for prayer and meditation, and also a place of temptation. Invite everyone to spend a few minutes writing in their journals about the "wilderness places" in their lives – the times of difficulty and crises and the places of peace and solitude.

For information on creating and using journals, see **Lenten Journaling** on page 124. Make an interesting design on your journal cover by sprinkling sand over top of white glue. Sand reminds us of the time Jesus spent in the desert before beginning his public ministry.

Closing Worship

Related Scripture Passages: Psalm 23:4, Isaiah 40:31, Acts 2:25-27a, 2 Cor. 4:8-9
Meditation: Read Margaret Fishback Powers' poem **Footprints** on page 27.
Scripture Prayer: *Photocopy and cut apart the **Comfort and Assurance** Scripture passages on the next page. Gather in a circle and give everyone one passage. Begin with these words:*

> Throughout the ages, people have turned to the Bible for comfort and assurance in times of difficulty. Some people memorize scripture passages they find especially encouraging. Then in difficult times, no matter where they are, they can remember these and draw strength and comfort from knowing God is present with them. We can imagine that Jesus drew comfort from the Scripture passages he knew, especially as he faced fears about his own death.

Invite everyone to read their passage silently and reflect on how it might relate to their own lives. Then one after another read the passages aloud as the closing prayer, ending with these words:

> Loving God, you know our struggles and our pain. Help us to know you are always present with us. Amen.

Take the Bible passages home to read for comfort in difficult times. Or give your passage to someone else if you think its message is particularly suited to that person.

Comfort and Assurance
Some Scripture Passages

 cut apart on lines

Those who trust in the Lord for help will find their strength renewed. They will rise on wings like eagles; they will run and not get weary; they will walk and not grow weak.

Isaiah 40:31

The Lord says, "Here is my servant, whom I strengthen – the one I have chosen, with whom I am pleased."

Isaiah 42:1

I am the Lord who created you; from the time you were born, I have helped you.

Isaiah 44:2

I have cared for you from the time you were born. I am your God and will take care of you until you are old and your hair is gray. I made you and will care for you; I will give you help and rescue you.

Isaiah 46:3b-4

Ask, and you will receive; seek, and you will find; knock, and the door will be opened to you.

Luke 11:9

I saw the Lord before me at all times. God is near me, and I will not be troubled. And so I am filled with gladness, and my words are full of joy. And I, mortal though I am, will rest assured in hope, because you will not abandon me in the world of the dead.

Acts 2:25-27a

God will wipe away all tears from their eyes. There will be no more death, no more grief or crying or pain.

Revelation 21:4

What we see now is like a dim image in a mirror; then we shall see face-to-face. What I know now is only partial; then it will be complete – as complete as God's knowledge of me.

1 Cor. 13:12

We are often troubled, but not crushed; sometimes in doubt, but never in despair; there are many enemies, but we are never without a friend; and though badly hurt at times, we are not destroyed.

2 Cor. 4:8-9

Even if I go through the deepest darkness, I will not be afraid, Lord, for you are with me.

Psalm 23:4

As I lie in bed, I remember you; all night long I think of you, because you have always been my help. In the shadow of your wings I sing for joy. I cling to you, and your hand keeps me safe.

Psalm 63:6-8

There are many rooms in my Father's house, and I am going to prepare a place for you. I would not tell you this if it were not so.

John 14:2

Adolescent Suicide

What causes a teenager to turn to suicide? It's rarely the result of one single factor. Usually it's a combination of things – some big, some little. Then it escalates to a point that suicide seems to be the only escape route. People with difficult problems and troubled histories respond in different ways. Some seem to have an inner resilience that helps them handle problems. Others find the same situations extremely difficult. It's important to look at each person individually. Many young people who appear "happy-go-lucky" are in fact struggling with enormous problems which they keep hidden.

What Are the Warning Signs?

While each of the following are warning signs that someone might be at risk of suicide, do not panic if you recognize one of them in a youth you know. Look for a cluster of clues in any one person. Some warning signs are:

- Sudden changes in behavior (e.g. eating and/or sleeping patterns, reversal of their "normal" character, increase in aggressive behavior, neglect of appearance, sudden withdrawal or unexplainable cheerfulness after a period of unhappiness).
- Complaints of feeling down or depressed.
- Marked change in school performance (e.g. difficulty concentrating, drop in marks).
- Substance abuse, or an increase in use if drugs and/or alcohol are already a problem.
- Withdrawal or isolation from friends, family, or social activities.
- Making final arrangements (e.g. giving away prized possessions).
- Previous suicide attempt – many people make an attempt before completing suicide.
- Suicide threats, notes, messages, preoccupation with suicide. These can be revealed through writing, drawings, and direct or indirect verbal expression.

What Can I Do?

If a youth talks to you about "feeling down" or you see some of the warning signs in a youth you know, here are some ideas about what you can do:

- Establish rapport with the person. Listen carefully but in a relaxed manner.
- Take time to explore what they are thinking and feeling. Ask direct questions (e.g. "Is something really bothering you? Are you thinking of hurting yourself?"). Try to identify what's stressing them the most.
- Refer them to a professional or community agency. Help them find resources. Talk to the clergy in your church.

Here are some ideas about what not to do:

- Don't panic because you have seen some warning signs. Keeping calm will help them not to panic.
- Don't cut the person off or ignore their need to talk about what's bothering them.
- Don't minimize their distress (e.g. "You're young. It'll pass." or "It can't be that bad." or "Don't be so serious.").
- Don't try to solve all their problems at once. Find out what the immediate problem is and help them see their way through it.
- Don't try to handle this on your own. Talk to youth or mental health professionals in your community and to the clergy in your church.

Identity and Self-Esteem

Group Check-in

If you were a character from a comic strip or an action hero, which would you be? Invite group members to share their ideas and explain why (e.g. I'd be Calvin from *Calvin and Hobbes* because I have a wild imagination and I'm always getting into trouble).

Personality Traits

How well do you know yourself? Exercises that help people identify their personality traits, characteristics, and preferences can be important for personal growth and development.

Older teens might want to take a personality test like the *Myers-Briggs Type Indicator* test (published by the Consulting Psychologists Press, Inc., 3803 E. Bayshore Road, Palo Alto, California 94303). This test consists of a set of about 125 questions. They are designed to help people discover how they look at things and how they make decisions. Possibly a member of your local congregation or a school counselor can administer and "score" the test. Ask what costs may be involved. Some shorter versions of the test may also be available. Check your local library for books about personality types to share with group members. Some books include descriptions of individual personality types, suggestions of the kinds of careers a person might enjoy and be successful doing, and how people with different preferences can relate to each other.

For youth of any age, there are books like *Psychology for Kids: 40 Fun Tests That Help You Learn about Yourself* (by Jonni Kincher, MN: Free Spirit Publishing, 1990). Such books have exercises that give group members interesting insights into their personalities. Check with your local library for books on this subject.

Making Masks

Make plaster bandage masks (see **Plaster Masks** on page 134). Invite everyone to decorate their masks with symbols of their true or inner selves, the things they think others see, and the things they think others don't always see at first glance. Decorate masks with thick or pre-mixed tempera paints for the best effect. Provide a variety of colors.

Hiding Behind a Mask

We often talk about "wearing masks" that hide our true feelings or identities. We all face pressures to conform – to fit in. We sometime feel we can't be "real," or be ourselves, with others. It may not be easy to discuss this in a large group. Have group members pair off to talk about the questions below. Alternatively, provide writing materials or journals and some time for individual, personal reflection.

- Do you reveal different parts of yourself to different people? Why?
- How do you think others see you? Is the "real you" different? In what ways?
- What are some of things about you that not everyone – perhaps only someone who is really close to you – knows?

Together talk about how your group can be a place where people can be themselves. Do people feel comfortable "being who they are" in the group? What risks are involved? Why is it important that this group be a place where people feel safe and can be themselves?

Self-Esteem Rating

Hand out slips of paper. Ask everyone to rate their own sense of self-esteem from 1 to 10 (10 for a very healthy sense of self-esteem and 1 for poor self-esteem). Collect the papers, mix them up, then spread them out on an imaginary continuum from 1-10. Did most people say they had high or low self-esteem? What affects your self-image and your self-esteem in positive ways? In negative ways?

Four Things about Me

Ask everyone to write the following things down on a slip of paper:

1. A future goal
2. Three positive, personal qualities
3. A place they'd like to visit
4. Something that's very important to them.

Collect, shuffle and number them. (Don't let the others see them because they may recognize each other's handwriting.) Hand out blank paper and ask everyone to put down the numbers 1-10 (or the number of group members there are). Read each of the slips aloud in chronological order without identifying whose it is. Ask group members to write (without any talking) the name of the person whose response they think it is beside the corresponding number on their page. Then read out the slips a second time asking everyone to register their guesses by voting for the person who they think wrote it. Even if people guess incorrectly it can be quite affirming! Identify the owners and award a prize for the most correct guesses.

Lenten Retreat

Develop a retreat program focused on "identity." Include some of these ideas:

- Mailbags. See **Affirmation Bags** on page 162
- Night Hike. If your retreat is in a camp setting, take a night **Trust Hike**. The leader carries a ashlight and group members hold hands, leading each other and being led. (*Note:* Trace your route ahead of time in the daylight to make sure the path is clear and safe enough for walking at night.)
- Masks. See **Paper Domino Masks** on page 103 or **Plaster Masks** on page 134.
- Simple Meals. In keeping with the traditions of Lent, try some simple, meatless dishes like those found on page 112.
- Worship. Hand out slips of paper and ask everyone to write things they would like to let go of (e.g. anger, jealousy). Burn these in a wood stove or fire pit as part of your closing. Follow the process used in **The Power of Words** on the next page.
- Personality exercises. Include time in your program to try some exercises that help people identify personality traits, characteristics, and preferences (see **Personality Traits** on the previous page).

Group Identity

Sometimes people identify us by the group we're in. What identity does your group have in the congregation? Is this different from the way you wish to be identified? Plan a Lenten event for your congregation that will let them learn more about your group (see **Planning Special Events for Lent** on page 135 and **Passover Seder** on page 136).

Closing Worship

Related Scripture Passages: Genesis 1:26-31, Matthew 18:1-5, 2 Corinthians 3:18
Meditation: See **The Power of Words** on the next page.

The Power of Words
(A Meditation)

Preparation
Hand out a slips of paper and pencils to group members. Place a lit candle and a container for burning papers in the center of the circle. Print the words of the response on newsprint.

Prayer

Leader: There are many words that have the power to diminish self-esteem.
There are the words **others** use to describe **us**,
        the words **we** use to describe **ourselves**,
        the words we say **about** others,
        the words we say **to** others.
We know the power that these words can have over our lives and over the lives of others.
Yet God's Word is one of acceptance and love, forgiveness and compassion.
It is God's Word we are called to share with others.
Sadly though, it is God's Word that we so often fail to share.

Response: We offer you these words that have power over us and pray that your Word might have new power in us and through us. Amen.

Process
Take time to re ect and to name a word that has power over you (e.g. thin, clumsy, stubborn) and write this word on your paper. Invite everyone, as they are ready, to come forward, light the edge of the paper from their candle, and place it in the container provided, saying the word out loud if they wish. Have the whole group read the response together after each person comes forward and lights the edge of their paper.

Plaster Masks

You will need: Gypsona bandages (about 3/4 roll per mask – these are available at pharmacies, medical supply stores, and doctors' offices), scissors, bowls, water, newsprint to cover the oor, towels, Vaseline, toilet paper squares, strips of material for tying back hair (or bobby pins and hair gel)
(**Note:** You will need approximately 25 minutes to make each mask. The masks require several hours to dry thoroughly enough to be painted or decorated.)

Instructions:

1. Ask everyone to get into pairs. It is important that they choose someone they really trust, as this exercise involves a level of risk.
2. Decide who will have their mask made first. That person should tie their hair back if necessary and lie on the oor (with newsprint spread underneath their head to catch drips).
3. Apply a generous amount of Vaseline to the face along the hairline and over the eyebrows and a small amount over the rest of the skin.
4. Fold two squares of toilet paper or tissue into quarters and place one over each eye (eyes should be closed).
5. Fold another square in half and place over the lips. This will ensure that no water or plaster leaks into the eyes or mouth and that eyelashes will not come in contact with the plaster.
6. Begin making the masks by laying strips of plaster bandage, dipped in water, over the face beginning with the forehead and eyebrows and working towards the chin. (Be careful not to let any of these overlap onto hair. Vaseline at the hairline, especially at the temples, will keep bandages from sticking to this hair.)
7. Smooth strips as you go. Overlap bandages somewhat so there are at least two layers. (You may want to put some reinforcing strips around the hairline, sides and chin as these will be places the mask will be held by when painting it later.)
8. Lay strips across the bridge of the nose but do not cover the nostrils. Check to see if people want their mouth covered. Some people have difficulty breathing well through their nose and won't want their mouth covered. In that case, do not cover the lips with tissue or place the bandages around the mouth. Never cover the nostrils.

     (**Note:** Plaster bandages dry quite quickly. Likely by the time you have completed the mask, parts on the top forehead will be almost dry, so don't count on going back to reinforce these at the end. Do this as you go.)
9. Remove the mask when it is dry enough. The mask is dry when it feels dry and hard to the touch (4-5 min. or longer depending on how thick the bandages were applied). They are removed easily by having the person wiggle the skin on their face (e.g. wrinkling the forehead, moving the nose) until the mask loosens and then gently lifting it off. If the mask appears stuck to any hair as you remove it, use a little clean water to remoisten the plaster around it.
10. Allow several hours for the masks to dry thoroughly before decorating or painting them.

Planning Special Events for Lent

Plan a congregational Lenten event for the purpose of education, fund raising, or simply to share in some fun and fellowship!

Lenten Scavenger Clue Hunt

Go out in small groups to gather these items and to find the answers to the questions. Participants may need the help of their Bibles. Award a prize to the first group to return with all (or the most) items and answers.

1. Thirty pieces of silver. Who paid Judas to betray Jesus?
2. Something purple. What other Church Year season sometimes uses the color purple?
3. The signatures of 12 disciples. What does the word "disciple" mean?
4. Fish. Name two disciples who were fishers before becoming followers of Christ.
5. Rope. Who gave the order for Jesus to be whipped?
6. Cross. Name one person who was there when Jesus was crucified.
7. Palm branch. What celebration brought Jesus and his disciples into Jerusalem the time Jesus was greeted by people waving palm branches?
8. A restaurant (take-out) menu. Name something Jesus and his friends would have eaten at the Last Supper.
9. A calendar. How many days long is the Season of Lent?

Lenten Fair

Adapt this to suit your group and congregation. Set up booths for the events in Holy Week.
- Palm Reading. A fortune teller looks into her crystal ball and tells the story of the palm parade.
- Donkey rides. Invite children to play pin the tail on the donkey or enjoy a donkey ride on the back of a group member or adult.
- Foot washing. Offer foot washing or massage.
- The Last Supper. Set up a concession stand serving "Passover meals $3 each."
- The Garden of Gethsemane. Organize a "plant shop."
- The Betrayal. Try a sponge toss – with the church staff volunteering to be the targets!

Lenten Fund-Raisers

Thirty Pieces of Silver Meal

Host a potluck dinner, a Shrove Tuesday pancake dinner, or a seder meal. Admission price: 30 pieces of silver. This is symbolic of the money Judas received for betraying Jesus to the Jewish authorities, and a reminder of our need for repentance. Use the money to cover costs or for a project the group wants to support.

Lenten Book of Meditations

Order copies of a Lenten book of meditations. Encourage members of the congregation to purchase these for use in their homes during Lent. Sell these at cost or for a small profit and donate the money to support an outreach project in your area.

Events for the Last Days of Lent

1. Join with another group of your church to organize a congregational seder meal (see **Passover Seder** on the next page).
2. Plan an **Easter Vigil** or **Sunrise Worship** (page 140). Combine it with a **40-Hour Fast** (see page 116).

Passover Seder

Experience the Passover. Thursday of Holy Week is called Maundy Thursday, or Holy Thursday. On this day, Christians recall the meal that Jesus ate with his disciples the night before his crucifixion. The description of the Last Supper given in the gospels is commonly held to be a record of the seder of the first night of the Jewish Passover. The bread which Jesus ate was likely the unleavened bread. The wine was that designated by the Jews for use on the first night of the Passover. The hymn sung by Jesus and his disciples after the meal was the *Hallel*, which is still sung by Jewish people on this night. The order of service for the seder ritual is called The Haggadah. While there are hundreds of versions, there is little variation in the standard text. Obtain a copy from your denominational book room, a bookstore specializing in Hebrew texts (in most major centers), or by "surfing the net." Some public libraries carry the book, *Keeping Passover – Everything You Need to Know to Bring the Ancient Tradition to Life and to Create Your Own Passover Celebration* (by Ira Steingroot, Harper Collins, 1995). This book lives up to its title, providing lots of interesting information including details about the seder foods, ritual actions and blessings, and corresponding "textual fragments."

Preparing the Seder Table

You will need: lamb, toothpicks, parsley, horseradish, matzoth (available in most major grocery stores), grape juice, haroset (see recipe), hard-boiled egg, basin and towel, candles, white napkins and tablecloth, copies of the Passover.

> **Haroset** (also spelled Haroses, Haroseth)
> In a bowl, grate 1/2 lemon. Add 1 cup (250ml) chopped apple, 1/4 cup (60mL) chopped walnuts or blanched almonds, 1 tsp. (5mL) honey, 1 tsp. (5mL) cinnamon. Add 1-2 Tbsp. (15-30mL) Passover wine or apple juice. Stir mixture together. If it is crumbly add more wine/juice.

Instructions: Set a long table (or several) with white linen tablecloth, plates, candles and cutlery. Follow the instructions for creating a seder plate of symbolic foods. You will likely only want to provide some samples of seder foods (e.g. small pieces of lamb skewered on toothpicks) as putting on a full meal could be quite expensive. Learn the simple tune of the "Kaddesh U'rehats" to teach others. Locate some Jewish folk music and learn the grapevine step. Don't be afraid to use your best china and silverware. In Jewish tradition this is a very festive occasion, second only perhaps to Purim in its lively mood, full of singing and dancing, eating and enjoying the company of family and friends.

The Tradition of the Seder

Passover is marked by observing the seder meal (usually twice) and eating Pesach foods – foods made without leaven (yeast). According to tradition, Passover begins on the 15th day of Nisan in the Hebrew calendar. On the evening following the thirteenth of Nisan, the head of the household makes the final preparation for Passover by searching for leaven throughout the house. Before the ceremony of searching for leaven begins, a candle is lit and a prayer recited. The leaven is gathered and wrapped securely and on the fourteenth day of Nisan, at about ten o'clock in the morning, all the leaven is burned.

Seder is Aramaic for the Hebrew word *erekh* meaning "order." The festival meal and home service observed on the first and second night of the Jewish Passover is called the "seder" because a certain order is always followed in observing the ritual. The ceremony of the seder meal includes the retelling of the Exodus story and the eating of foods that symbolize both the slavery and deliverance out of slavery the Hebrew people experienced. This custom is according to the scriptural command at Exodus 13: 8: "When the festival begins, explain to your sons that you do all this because of what the Lord did for you when you left Egypt."

Section E: Season of Easter

Mood and Flavor of the Season

Easter is the oldest festival of the Church and the focal point of the Christian Year. The early Church celebrated Easter long before observing the Seasons of Lent or Christmas. The Season of Easter, or the "Great 50 Days," begins on Easter Sunday and continues until Pentecost, 50 days later. The Sundays of this season are called the Sundays of Easter. The liturgical colors of white and gold reflect the joy of this season.

During the Season of Easter we read stories of Jesus' appearances to the disciples after the Resurrection. As the disciples experienced Jesus with them in various places, the "good news" of Easter gradually dawned on them. We also read stories from the book of Acts about the Church's beginning and the spread of the Christian faith. Throughout this season we balance the disciples' gradual and growing awareness in the Gospels with the disciples' bold words and actions following Pentecost.

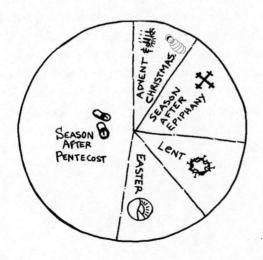

Special Days

Forty days after Easter Sunday Jesus ascended into heaven. We normally celebrate this on the Sunday nearest to Ascension Day. On Earth Day or Rogation Sunday, many congregations focus on concern for the environment. Rogation Sunday is normally celebrated on the Sunday preceding Ascension Day. The name comes from the Latin "rogare" meaning "to beg" or "to ask." Traditionally it was a special time of prayer and blessing of the spring crops. The English emphasized seed time, planting, and prayers for a bountiful harvest. Open-air services, processions through the fields and farms, and "beating the bounds" or walking the boundaries of the parish marked the observance.

Although not part of the Christian Year, many churches celebrate the second Sunday in May as Christian Family Sunday, the day secular society calls Mother's Day. On this day many denominations emphasize living in harmony – not only with our parents and siblings, but also with all God's children who are our brothers and sisters.

The Day of Pentecost, the last Sunday of the Easter Season, is a festival of fire and wind and the Holy Spirit. Vivid red, the liturgical color for this day, signifies the "tongues of fire" that rested on each disciple. The fire transformed the followers of Jesus (disciples) into the bearers of the message (apostles), who were "sent forth." Red is also the color of martyrdom, reminding us about the deaths of many early Christians.

On the Day of Pentecost we celebrate not only the Holy Spirit poured out on the disciples, but also God's Spirit at work today and the gifts of the Spirit in each of us.

Pentecost existed before the early church. Fifty days after the Jewish festival of Passover came the spring harvest festival of Pentecost, or the "Feast of Weeks." Greek-speaking Jews named the festival using the Greek word meaning "fiftieth." This celebration marked the end of the grain harvest and the beginning of the season of first fruits. In May, farmers harvested the wheat planted in November. Before the people ate any of the newly harvested crop, they dedicated it to God. Each family made two loaves from the new wheat, baked the bread according to laws, (found in the Book of Leviticus), and presented it as an offering at the temple. Today Jewish people usually refer to the Feast of Weeks as "Shavuot." At this Jewish festival Jewish boys and girls are confirmed ("Bar Mitzvah" and "Bat Mitzvah"). For Christians, Pentecost is also a time for Baptism, as described in Acts, and for Confirmation – the affirmation of baptismal faith.

Implications for Youth Ministry

Every year on the second Sunday of Easter, the lectionary reading includes the story of "doubting Thomas" – the disciple who was absent when Jesus first appeared to the disciples in the upper room. Thomas refused to believe that Christ had risen until he had seen him for himself (John 20:24-29). This story can be very meaningful for adolescents who engage in similar questioning about their beliefs and values. Use this story as a discussion starter about the questions and doubts of the youth in the group. Youth might enjoy interviewing some older members of the congregation and asking them about their beliefs, questions, and doubts.

The focus on the spread of the Christian faith and beginning of the early Church with the apostles, provide many possibilities for youth groups. Do the youth want to undertake a research project about how their congregation (or denomination) began? Consider visiting churches of other denominations to experience the variety and diversity within the Christian tradition.

The environment and community are also important themes for youth. They may want to participate in special Earth Day observances or lead an intergenerational service focused on concern for the environment. Does the group want to plan a retreat? Use this as an opportunity to reflect on experiences of early Christians who lived in community.

At this time of year they look back on the past year, and they may look forward to personal plans that will scatter them out into the world, like the apostles scattered after Pentecost. If the youth do not meet during the summer, plan how you will bring closure to the group. Gather and share information on summer services, leadership training, or camping opportunities for youth.

Idea Page #1   Life after Death

Group Check-in

Imagine that you have just been told that you have only three days to live. What would you do with those three days? Have everyone think about this; and then turn and share their ideas with the person next to them. Discuss (in pairs or in a group) what they know about the last three days of Jesus' life. What did he do? How is this similar or different from what you would do?

Sanctuary Sleepover

Plan a sleepover with games that can be done in your church's sanctuary (worship area). See the ideas on this page. Sleep in the sanctuary overnight and plan an evening worship and sunrise service around "tomb" experiences.

Sanctuary Games

1. Sanctuary Scavenger Hunt

Create a list that includes things or questions like how many banners or organ pipes there are in your sanctuary. Divide into teams. Award a prize for the first team to complete the list, the team that is most accurate, the team that doesn't know what an altar is, and so on.

2. Sanctuary Clue Hunt

This game will help familiarize everyone with your church's sanctuary (see page 142).

3. Pew Races

Everyone (including the leader) stands along the last (back) pew and receives a coin. On the leader's signal everyone ips their coin. The leader calls out whether it's heads or tails. All those who ipped the same thing move ahead one pew. Play continues as quickly as possible. The winner is the one who reaches the front row of pews first **and** ips the correct coin. Make the game even wilder by calling "over," "under," or "around" after each ip. In order to move forward players must do as the leader says (e.g. crawl under the pew).

A Sanctuary or a Tomb?

The word sanctuary comes from the Latin "*sanctuarium*" meaning "holy place." It can describe the actual place or room in the church where people gather to worship or, in a broader sense, the church itself.

When early Christians feared being persecuted by the Romans, they gathered in secret to worship, often in tombs (catacombs). Later, Christians were free to practice their religion and began to build places for worship. Today we believe that the architectural feature of a tomb-like shape was intentionally incorporated into the design of early church buildings.

In church buildings today, the sanctuary comes in all shapes and sizes and is only one of many rooms. But sanctuaries are still meant to remind us of the early Christian gatherings in addition to our own rebirth each time we go out after worship. Like the empty tomb, the sanctuary remains a powerful symbol of Jesus' death and resurrection.

Easter Word Association

Photocopy pages 143-144, mount on cardboard backing if you wish, and cut apart the squares. Divide into two teams. Without looking, one player takes a card. They must get the rest of the team to guess correctly (in 30 seconds) the word printed at the top of the card **without** using any of the other words printed on the card. Whole sentences are O.K. but don't include any of the words on the card. If the player does, they are disqualified and it's the other team's turn. When all the cards are used, discuss the words and their connection with Easter.

Paschal Candles

You will need: large white candles (3in.(7.5cm) in diameter or larger), stylus tool or skewer/toothpicks, felt-tipped pen, five whole cloves

Instructions: Trace a design in the wax, with a cross as the central symbol. Include the first and last letters of the Greek alphabet – the alpha and omega – which are symbols for God, who is "the beginning and the end" (Rev. 1:8). Carve the design using a stylus or skewer. Fill in the design with colored wax by holding the end of a wax crayon (peel the paper off first) over the design. Melt it with a match or candle, allowing the wax to drip into the carved out sections. When the wax is cool, scrape off any that dripped outside the design. Insert the five cloves into the cross, one at each point and one in the center. These symbolize the wounds to Jesus' hands, feet, and side. Inscribe the date on the candle.

Easter Vigil or Sunrise Worship

Gather Saturday evening or in the early hours before dawn to wait for the first light of Easter morning. Celebrate the joy of the Resurrection together through music, food, and dramatic readings.

Easter Vigils probably began as a commemoration of the vigil the first disciples kept. Because Jewish laws forbade work on the Sabbath, the disciples were unable to prepare Jesus' body as they had hoped. They kept vigil, waiting for daybreak on Sunday (the end of the Sabbath). When the women arrived at the tomb to prepare his body, they found the tomb empty.

The Custom of Candles at Easter

In some countries it is customary to completely darken the church Good Friday. Then just before sunrise on Easter Sunday the clergy lights the Paschal or Christ candle "with new fire." As worshipers arrive at church they are given candles that they light from the Paschal candle.

On Easter morning in France, it is still traditional for families to take home candles that have been blessed at church. These are used only on special occasions throughout the year, lasting until the following Easter.

Seven Last Words of Christ

Provide paper or make journals (see **Lenten Journaling** on page 124) and some quiet time for reflecting on the passages below. Although these are phrases, they are commonly known as "The Seven Last Words of Christ."

1. "Father, forgive them, for they do not know what they are doing." Luke 23:34
2. "I tell you the truth, today you will be with me in paradise." Luke 23:43
3. "Dear woman, here is your son...Here is your mother." John 19:26-27
4. "My God, my God, why have you forsaken me?" Matthew 27:46
5. "I am thirsty." John 19:28
6. "It is finished." John 19:30
7. "Father, into your hands I commit my spirit." Luke 23:46

Closing Worship

Related Scripture Passages: Matthew 28:1-10, Luke 24:45-52, John 5:24, 2 Cor. 4:10,14,18
Responsive Reading: Read **Easter Sunday** on the next page.

Easter Sunday
A Responsive Reading
(based on John 20:1-2)

Hand out candles to everyone and place a large candle before the group.

Leader: It was about three o'clock on Friday afternoon when Jesus died.

ALL: And the world was dark and silent.

Leader: Some friends of Jesus came and took his body, wrapped it in a linen cloth and laid it in a tomb.

ALL: And the tomb was dark and silent.

Leader: Early on Sunday morning some women went to the tomb. They brought with them oil and spices to anoint Jesus' body. It was early, before the sun had even risen.

ALL: And the world was dark and silent.

Leader: But when they arrived at the tomb they found the stone that had been placed over the entrance had been rolled away. And when they entered the tomb they could not find Jesus' body.

ALL: The tomb was dark and silent.

Leader: So they ran away and told the others, "They have taken the Lord from the tomb, and we don't know where they have put him!"

(Light the Christ candle. Invite others to light their candles from it.)

Leader: Christ is risen!

ALL: He is risen indeed! Alleluia!

Sanctuary Clue Hunt

Instructions:

Write the suggested clues on slips of paper (add others if you wish). Place all but the first one in the appropriate spots around the sanctuary. Begin by reading out the first clue. When someone locates that object, they will find the next clue, and so on. For example, Clue #2 would be taped somewhere on the lectern where the person reading the scripture usually stands. This clue will instruct them to find Clue #3 in a different location and so on. The final clue might lead the group to a place where you will have your next activity.

Suggested Clues:

1. Known as a "lectern," this is where the person reading scripture usually stands. (lectern)
2. This entryway to the sanctuary is sometimes called the "narthex." (narthex or outer sanctuary)
3. This is where the choir sits. (choir loft)
4. When the minister is delivering the sermon you might find a glass of water here. (under the pulpit)
5. This is where the Bible and Christ candle, and sometimes owers, are placed. (altar)
6. Referred to as a "font," this is filled with water for Baptism. (baptismal font)
7. People can look at this to find hymn numbers. (hymn boards)
8. This instrument accompanies most of the hymns we sing. (organ/piano)
9. The children usually sit here during the Children's Time. (steps/front of the church)
10. This is the doorway choir members usually enter through. (a doorway into the sanctuary)
11. This is where people in wheelchairs would enter the sanctuary. (wheelchair access/ramp)
12. This is where the minister stands to deliver the benediction. (front of the sanctuary/steps)

Make up your own version of the game with the clue hunt going beyond the sanctuary into other spaces in the church.

ROBBER

thief	money
steal	burglar
jail	

CRUCIFIXION

cross	Good Friday
death	Easter
Jesus	

WINE

red	blood
drink	Communion
alcohol	

RESURRECTION

Easter	tomb
alive	crucifixion
Jesus	

ANGEL

wings	guardian
fly	halo
Heaven	

SPICES

food	body
taste	Mary Magdalene
anoint	

EASTER

Resurrection	
Jesus	Good Friday
Sunday	morning

BUTTERFLY

wings	colorful
cocoon	caterpillar
insect	

CHICK

baby	peep
fuzzy	egg
yellow	

LAMB

wool	curly
sheep	sacrificial
baby	

(continued on next page)

NAILS

hammer   palms

pound   sharp

Jesus

SUNRISE

morning   dark

light   wake

colors

JUDAS

traitor   betray

disciples   Jesus

silver coins

ROOSTER

crows   Peter

chicken   deny

three

TOMB

empty   grave

Joseph of Arimathea

stone   body

MARY

Magdalene   Easter

friend   disciple

Jesus

DISCIPLE

friend   twelve

Jesus   group

follower

GARDEN OF GETHSEMANE

disciples   pray

sleep   arrest

Jesus

LILY

flower   smells

Easter   pure

white

COMMUNION

meal   Eucharist

bread   Last Supper

wine

The Early Church

Group Check-in

It was a dangerous thing to be a Christian in the early church. Christians held meetings in secret and used a secret sign – like a secret handshake – to identify themselves to each other. They wrote and read books written in "code," like the Book of Revelation. In order to remain anonymous, it is believed that the author of this book assumed the name "John" (Revelation 1:9). Many authors do this today. Ask everyone to introduce themselves using a pseudonym – their names pronounced backwards can often produce hilarious results!

Secret Meeting

The early Church suffered much persecution at the hands of the Roman government. Christians took many risks in meeting as a community of believers and did so with the greatest of secrecy. Often Christians met in underground tombs (catacombs). Plan to have a meeting in a "secret" location – perhaps the church basement, a small room, or the sanctuary. How will you inform group members of the secret location? Here are some ideas:

- Set up a grapevine. Provide everyone with a list of group members' phone numbers. Explain that you will start the grapevine by phoning the first name on the list and telling that person the location. That person will pass the information along to the next person on the list and so on.
- Put a message (in code of course!) in the bulletin the Sunday before the meeting is to take place.
- Invite group members to come to the church at the regular meeting time, but don't tell them where in the church you will be meeting. Use the sign of the fish to lead them to your secret location.

Picture Code

When people in the early Church met others – in the marketplace, drawing water at a communal well – they would draw half a fish in the sand with a walking stick or their foot. If the other person was also a Christian, they would respond by drawing the other half. Divide the group into several teams to play this game. Have them convey messages to their team members by drawing them. The first team member who thinks they know the message whispers it to the person drawing. If they're correct, they complete the drawing (or write out the message). Think of some messages ahead of time and write these on slips of paper.

The Symbol of the Fish

Sometime in the early Church life, the figure of a fish took symbolic value as the sign of Christ. The acrostic derived from the Greek letters of the word "fish" (ichthys) were understood to stand for the Greek words for "Jesus [i] Christ [ch], God's [th] Son [y], Savior [s]" and the use of the symbol persists to this day in Christian iconography.

Agape Meal

Have an agape meal together.

Agape meals were the "love feasts" of the early Christians – meals provided by church members for religious fellowship and especially for charity to the poor and widows in their community. The custom originates from the earliest days of the Church and is described in the Book of Acts. Maybe it was rooted in the common meals Jesus ate with his disciples, or from various instances in his ministry as when he fed the multitude (Mark 6:34-44, 8:1-9).

Promoting Community

Early Christians shared many meals (see above) and as a result, believers felt a sense of community. In what ways does our church promote fellowship? (e.g. coffee hour following worship, potluck dinners, church picnic) Which of these interests you the most? What other ideas do you have? List all of the ideas on newsprint. With what committee in your church could these ideas be shared?

Fellowship

Use group members' imagination and energy to do something that promotes fellowship in your congregation:

- Plan a congregational dinner
- Organize games for the church picnic
- Host coffee hour (or "lemonade on the lawn" one warm Sunday morning)
- Create a photo directory or "Our Church Family" wall with pictures to help people get to know one another

Christians and Romans

A new spin on **Sardines** (see page 22)! Add this variation. Each player gets three cards with the sign of the fish printed on them. Explain that if they are caught meeting with other Christians (i.e. in the hiding place) by a Roman officer they must give up one of these cards. These cards allow a player to remain in the game. Once a player gives up all of these, they are out of the game. One player is "It" and goes off to hide in a "meeting spot." Other group members sit in a circle and close their eyes. As you walk around the circle, tap someone on the shoulder (or two people depending on the size of your group). That person becomes an undercover Roman officer. The object of the game is for players to find the meeting spot without tipping off the Romans.

Game Rules:

1. Roman officers cannot follow one player around for more than one minute.
2. If the Roman officer catches players in a meeting place (or entering it) each player must give up one fish card and a new game begins.
3. If the Roman officer finds the meeting place before everyone finds it they become "It" for the next round and hide in a meeting spot.
4. The game is won when all of the group members find the meeting spot safely without being caught by the Romans.

History of the Early Church

Learn more about the early Church while overcoming obstacles in this cooperative game. See Section F for the game board, cards, and instructions.

Closing Worship

Related Scripture Passages: Acts 2:42, 46, Acts 20:7-11, 1 Corinthians 11:20

Group Sharing: Phone everyone ahead of time and ask them to bring a symbol of a community they belong to (e.g. sports team, club, circle of school friends). Gather in the "meeting spot" (if you played **Christians and Romans** above) or in a secret location. Darken the room and light candles. Take turns presenting symbols and explaining their significance, and then placing them in the center of the circle.

Prayer: Thank you God for this Christian community in which we are all members. Be with us as we return now to our other communities – our homes, our friends, our schools. Amen.

Idea Page #3 Community Living

Group Check-in

How energetic is everyone feeling? Ask group members to stand on an imaginary continuum line from high to low energy. Encourage everyone to notice where others are standing. Take some time to think about how all of us might be sensitive to the energy levels of others. How might this affect how you relate or interact with each other at this group gathering?

Group as Community

Plan a sleepover or a group breakfast to help the youth experience living in community. Use ideas from this page to plan activities for your time together.

Reflection on Living in Community

The Book of Acts describes how the early Christians lived and worked together, sharing their belongings, eating meals, and worshiping together (read Acts 2:42-47, 4:32-35). Recall a time when you had this type of experience with a group of people – at a retreat, camp, group sleepover. Use the following questions to guide a reflection on the experience.

- How was the experience similar to the community living of early Christians? What did you really enjoy about the experience?
- Were there any problems or difficulties?
- Would you like to live like this every day?
- How did you feel about how the work was shared?
- Who took responsibility for making sure everyone was included?
- How were problems solved?
- Did you like the way time was spent?
- What advantages are there to living in community? What disadvantages?
- Considering the description of the early Christian community in Acts, would you want to belong to it? What would be the advantages? The disadvantages?

Communal Living

Read the description of the early Christian community in Acts 2:42-47, 4:32-35. Even today there are communities that follow this model. Ask the youth to name any groups they are aware of that live like this and what they know about them. Share the information from **Living in Community** on page 150. Then reflect on the following questions:

- How are these groups similar to the early Christian community? How are they different?
- Why do you think people would choose to live in a community setting like this? What advantages would there be?
- If you were to join one of these communities, what would be the signs for you that this is a healthy place for you to be? (e.g. people respect your feelings, you can disagree with leaders, you can come and go as you want.)

Signs of Healthy Community

List at least five "signs of a healthy community." If you have a large group, divide into smaller groups to brainstorm. Return to the larger group to share ideas. Take a vote to determine which ideas are considered most important for a healthy community. In what ways is your group a community? If you created "standards" at the beginning of the year, look at these. How do they reflect the qualities just identified as important for a healthy community?

Healthy and Unhealthy Communities

Hold a 3-step discussion about communities.

1) Our Church as Community: We in the church are a community of believers like the early Christians were. Like them we share meals together (the Lord's Supper), share our possessions and support those in need (through our offering), and worship together. Why do you think people come to church? What are they seeking? Brainstorm a list of reasons people might want to be part of a community like the Church.

2) Cult Communities: In recent years there have been a number of community living situations – often referred to as "cults"– that have ended in tragedy. Ask the group to name some and share what they know about them. Although the word cult has mostly negative connotations today, it comes from the Latin "cultus," meaning "worship." Disturbingly, many of these groups claim to take the early Christian community as their model with its principles of love for others, shared belongings and responsibilities, eating and worshiping together. Use the information from **Sects or Cults?** on the next page to discuss why a person might get involved in a cult.

3) Compare and Discuss: Look at your list of reasons for people wanting to belong to the Church. How are these different from the reasons a person might have for getting involved in a cult? How do you tell the difference between a healthy and unhealthy community?

Community Assessment

How does your congregation promote community? Complete the **Community Assessment Form** on page 151 together or in pairs. Then look at the key and discuss the questions included with the ratings.

Promoting a Sense of Community

Do group members think the congregation does enough to encourage community among its members? How are people of different ages made to feel a part of the community? Plan to do something for your congregation that will promote a sense of community. See **Fellowship** on page 146 for some ideas.

Catacomb

Choose a small, cave-like spot. Darken the room and light some candles to create atmosphere. Play **Sardines** (see page 22 for rules). You be "It." Instruct the youth to wait while you go to the secret location. After a couple of minutes they can begin looking for you. When everyone has found the spot, have your closing worship in this secret "catacomb," re-enacting the way early Christians worshipped in secrecy (see **Secret Meeting** on page 145).

> *Nobody joins a cult. People join groups that answer their questions, or meet their needs...for friends, family, support. People want to believe in something that will give them this magical recipe for success or happiness, or being closer to God.*
>
> —A leader in cult research

Closing Worship

Related Scripture Passages: Acts 2:42-47, Acts 4:32-35

Community Sharing: When early Christians met to worship together they would often read from the "Torah" or Hebrew Scriptures, retell stories of Jesus' teachings and miracles, talk about the way God wanted them to live, pray, and share a ritual meal of bread and wine together "in remembrance" of Jesus. Retell or read a favorite passage from the Hebrew Scripture and from one of the Gospels. What do they teach us about God's way? Say a prayer or grace and share some bread, grape juice, or other food. (If your tradition requires an ordained minister to administer communion elements, remind the youth that this is not Communion or Eucharist. This may spark some interesting conversation and questions for your minister to answer.)

Sects or Cults?

The two terms are often used in talking about religious groups that are not in the main stream of religious life. The terms are "sect" and "cult." The term "sect" properly refers to a religious group that is an offshoot or splinter group of a larger, usually more orthodox, church. Many modern churches started as sects of a larger church. These splinter groups are usually concerned with reforming or reviving the parent religion.

In this sense, the Branch Davidians are a sect, as they have their roots in the Seventh-Day Adventist Church. (As you might remember, a group of 85 Branch Davidians, and their leader, David Koresh, perished in Waco, Texas, in 1993.) This group of Branch Davidians were living in communal setting, in a barracks-like commune (known as Ranch Apocalypse) outside of the little town of Waco. But some would also say that the Branch Davidians were a "cult."

What's the difference?

The difference lies not in what the group believes but how it behaves. Cults often are very authoritarian and idealize their leaders. For example, the Unification Church (the followers of which are commonly referred to as "Moonies" after their leader Rev. Sun Myung Moon) organize themselves as alternative "families." The Rev. Sun Myung Moon and his wife are referred to as the Perfect Parents. Similarly, David Koresh was a father figure with incredible power to most Branch Davidians. In the Church Universal and Triumphant, leader Elizabeth Clare Prophet's followers call her Guru Ma. These new religious "families" replace the members' real families. Many members become cut off from their families because of the rules of the organization or because their new religious beliefs come to be at odds with those of their relatives.

Rabbi Michael Skobac, who works with Jewish students at the University of Toronto, explains why those who are working in the cult-watching field don't apply the term "cult" to a religious movement on the basis of its beliefs but rather on the way it behaves. In the way a group "proselytizes" or converts people to its beliefs and in the way it forms its members into a group, you can see signs of a healthy or unhealthy community. If it uses manipulative tactics, discourages critical thinking and frowns upon personal freedom, the community may be one that could be called a cult. Aggressive recruiting is one of the characteristics of these new movements, but other signs include: an authoritarian, usually charismatic leader who demands loyalty and unquestioning obedience to his or her leadership; a set of beliefs or practices, different from the dominant culture, that puts the group in opposition to established churches, institutions, and governments; a claim to being persecuted by the outside world; a claim to hold the exclusive truth; requiring members to conform to certain rules on fear of discipline or excommunication; avoidance of any significant interaction with other religious groups or people "outside" the group; avoidance of paid clergy or professional religious workers and instead an emphasis on the role of lay (non-ordained) people.

The difficulty for many Christians is that some of these characteristics – the charismatic leaders, the beliefs different from the dominant culture, the sense of persecution from the outside world, and the claim to hold exclusive truth – were all realities in the early Church. What kept Christianity from being a cult was perhaps the variety of ways early Christians organized themselves and shared their faith. Being willing to disagree with one another and to allow for some freedom "in the Spirit" allowed the new faith to develop in healthy ways.

Some information from "Cults or Faith on the Fringe?" by Mike Milne, *The United Church Observer*, April 1994.

Living In Community

Sojourners

The Sojourners community live and work in inner-city Washington, D.C., reaching out to those who are marginalized – people living on the streets, those living in poverty, in shelters, those who are suffering addictions to drugs and alcohol, the unemployed. The message of Sojourners is both prophetic and simple:

There must be a radical connection between our faith and finances, between our piety and politics, between our salvation and the streets.

Sojourners staff members have made a commitment to live simply and in solidarity with poor people. The base salary of staff members is $18,000 (U.S.) and the highest salary allowed is $24,000 (U.S.). Regardless of a person's position in the organization or the length of years they've been working in the community, Sojourners believe that all people involved in the ministry bring equally valuable gifts to the whole. The mission statement of Sojourners is taken from the Bible: "And what does the Lord require of you? To act justly, to love mercy, and to walk humbly with your God." (Micah 6:8)

In order to help people understand how Christians must address issues of social justice, the community produces a magazine (called "Sojourners") which informs people about all kinds of justice issues in North America and around the world. This is just one way the Sojourners community advocates for the rights of the poor and marginalized.

L'Arche

L'Arche was started in 1964 by a French-Canadian, Jean Vanier. He wanted to provide a home setting, rather than an institution, for adults with mental disabilities. L'Arche is a French word for "the ark" and Vanier wanted L'Arche homes to be safe places for people who are mentally handicapped. Such people often need the refuge the ark symbolizes.

Some L'Arche folk have trouble dressing or feeding themselves, while others are able to work at some jobs. Some may not be able to read or talk very well. If these people are developmentally handicapped, what can they teach the rest of us? "Love, forgiveness, humility, and the celebration of life" says Jeff Moore, who with his wife Debbie worked at the L'Arche house in Wolfville, Nova Scotia, called "Homefires." The people who live in the house spend time together, care about each other, eat their meals together, do their household jobs and try to live together joyfully. Like a family.

There are 28 houses like this in Canada, and over 100 around the world. They are busy teaching people like you and me how to love one another, how not to rush too much, and how to put the people you love before anything else.

Doukhobors

The Doukhobors developed in 17th century Russia. Believing that it was wrong to use the icons, ceremonies, and religious symbols of the 17th century Russian State Church, a group of people, under the leadership of Peter W. Verigin, found in the simple teachings of Jesus Christ the religious freedom they wanted—the freedom to worship God "in spirit and in truth." These teachings led them to the conviction that violence and wars were wrong. This eventually got them into a lot of trouble with the Russian government because they refused to be in the army or fight in wars. Many of them were imprisoned and died for their beliefs; others were exiled to Siberia, including their leader Peter Verigin.

The plight of the Doukhobors was not unnoticed by other Christians. Helped by Leo Tolstoy, a Russian Christian philosopher, and groups such as the Quakers, they were released from Russia and allowed to travel to Canada. The Doukhobors immigrated to Canada with full religious privileges, including exemption from military service. Many went to live and farm together on the prairies. Originally, all Doukhobors lived in a communal manner, with smaller houses surrounding one large brick house. The large house served as common dining-room, kitchen, and worship area. (During the Depression years, for instance, Doukhobors showed much kindness to many homeless and unemployed Canadians.)

Underlying the whole Doukhobor life and economy is the religious basis upon which it is built. The whole teaching of the Doukhobors is permeated with the gospel spirit of love. Worship is simple – commencing with the singing of the Lord's Prayer followed by psalms and prayers (also sung in most cases). Sometimes these are followed by a message, given by a member or visitor, who takes their place behind a small table with the simple elements of bread, salt, and water – signifying Jesus, the bread and water of life, and people, the salt of the earth. Other than this there are no outward forms, such as other sacraments, crucifixes, images or stained-glass windows, in their worship.

Community Assessment Form

Assess how your congregation promotes "community." Check off as many boxes as apply, add up the total and see the key at the bottom of the page for result.

Our congregation

___ frequently has potluck dinners or intergenerational (all ages) events

___ has a time of fellowship (coffee hour) following worship regularly

___ serves juice, soda pop or other beverages for children, youth and those who don't drink coffee (if your church has a fellowship time following worship)

___ promotes or supports programs that make links between the church and local community (e.g. outreach programs)

___ has a church school

___ has Bible study programs for adults

___ has mid-week programs for young people (e.g. youth group, Scouts)

___ encourages people to wear name tags to help people get to know one another (if your congregation is fairly large)

___ has a congregational photo or phone directory available to members

___ has a committee responsible for sponsoring parish events, retreats, fellowship meals, etc.

___ has a process for acknowledging newcomers and visitors to the congregation on Sunday mornings

___ holds occasional "newcomer gatherings" to help people meet one another and learn about the congregation/parish

___ has greeters/ushers to greet people at the door prior to worship

___ passes "the peace" during the worship service

___ publishes a newsletter to keep members informed about congregational life

___ informs people of upcoming events/activities at the church (e.g. through bulletin, information board. etc)

___ has a "telephone tree" to get information or concerns quickly to people

___ reaches out to seniors and shut-ins who are unable to attend church services (e.g. through audio or video tapes of sermons or worship services, at home visitors, Seniors' teas, etc.)

___ has a Visitation (or other committee) that visits homes of church members, the hospitalized or shut-ins

---

Key:

15-19   Your congregation works hard to foster a sense of community between its members. What were the items you didn't check off? Do you think these are good ideas? Is there something your group can do to nurture community in the congregation?

10-15   The sense of community in your congregation must be growing! What were the items you didn't check off? Were there ideas you'd never thought of before? Maybe your group could write a letter or make a presentation to the appropriate people or committee in your church suggesting one of these as a way of nurturing community within the congregation. Or perhaps there's something you can do as a group (e.g. plan a potluck dinner, help with the newsletter)?

1-10   You've made a good start at promoting a sense of community among the members of the congregation. Look at the items you didn't check off. How might these things promote a sense of community in your church? Are any of these suggestions your group might undertake together? Perhaps you might write a letter or make a presentation to the appropriate people or committee in your church about one of these suggestions (e.g. to make or order name tags for members, to have a photo directory made). Plan a fund raiser to help cover any costs.

Easter and Pentecost Symbols

Easter symbols remind us of new life, the resurrection, the glory of the risen Christ, and a new dawn in our own lives.

Pentecost symbols remind us of the coming of the Holy Spirit, and our being touched and filled by the Holy Spirit.

Idea Page #4 # Environment

Group Check-in

Ask everyone to think of the name of their favorite tree. Take turns using gestures and pantomime, but no words, to elicit the name from others. Afterwards everyone can share what they know about their tree-mendous trees!

Creation Stories

Compare the Creation story in Genesis in different translations of the Bible or look at some Creation stories from other cultures, such as Native North American. What are the similarities? What are the differences? What was God's intention in creating people?

Creation in Drama

Read dramatically **The Genesis Story**, on page 155. Compare it with the version you know or look up the story in the Bible. What are the differences between them? What is significant to you about God creating people after the rest of Creation? Do you know other versions? Do some of them describe God creating the plants, birds and other animals before creating humans? What do Creation stories suggest about God's plan for the relationship between people and the rest of Creation?

Creation Symbols in Worship

- Decorate the sanctuary. Make tie-dyed or fabric-painted banners or create a papier mâché globe. Use a round balloon and suspend it from the ceiling (modify the instructions for a **Piñata** on page 103).
- Create special T-shirts for group members to wear at a worship service (see page 159 for suggestions).
- Include recycling boxes, ags representing the four directions (black, yellow, white, red), masks, a Bible, a globe, as decorations or elements to be presented at the beginning of worship.

Creation Stories

Use some of your own ideas and some of the suggestions on these pages to plan a worship service on the Creation theme.

Prayer and the Environment

Here are some ideas for writing or locating prayers that focus on the environment:

- Choose a favorite from *Earth Prayers from Around the World: 365 Prayers, Poems, and Invocations for Honoring the Earth*, San Francisco: Harper Collins, 1991.
- Write prayers to accompany slide projected images. One group took pictures of buses, traffic, and a ferry terminal in their city. As slides were projected on a wall, one group member read this prayer:

    "Creator, our lives are made faster with cars, buses, ferries, and planes. The air is being polluted with our vehicles and we speed quickly past, ignoring the destruction. We are thankful for things like car pooling and cycling paths, and pray that we may slow down and strive to change our polluting ways."

- Pray using the poem **The Right to Dream** on page 158, inviting everyone to add their own "dreams" for the environment.
- Read **Teach Us and Show Us God's Way** on page 157 or the closing prayer on the next page. Then as a group, choose an environmental focus and brainstorm sentences for your own prayer.

Creation Bulletin Board

Design a special bulletin board or cover for the order of worship. Include information about actions individuals can take to protect the environment. Research the subject using books like *The Canadian Green Consumer Guide,** Toronto: McLelland & Stewart, 1989 and *50 Simple Things You Can Do to Save the Earth*, Berkeley, CA: Earthworks Press, 1989.

*Also published in the U.K. as the *Green Consumer Guide.*

Celtic Blessing

Use this prayer as a benediction for the closing of a meeting or a worship service:

Deep peace of the running wave to you;
Deep peace of the owing air to you;
Deep peace of the quiet earth to you;
Deep peace of the swirling stars to you;
Deep peace of the God of peace to you;
Deep peace to you. Amen.

Closing Worship

Related Scripture Passages: Genesis 3:1-13, Job 26:5-14, Psalm 96, Psalm 104
Prayer: Read the following prayer in unison or have everyone take turns reading a sentence.

A Native American Prayer

Every part of this earth is sacred.
Every shining pine needle, every sandy shore, every mist in the dark woods,
every clearing and humming insect is holy.
The rocky crest, the juices of the meadow,
the beasts and all the people, all belong to the same family.
Teach your children that the earth is our mother.
Whatever befalls the earth befalls the children of the earth.
We are part of the earth, and the earth is a part of us.
The rivers are our brothers, they quench our thirst.
The perfumed owers are our sisters,
the air is precious, for all of us share the same breath.
The wind that gave our grandparents breath also receives their last sigh.
The wind gave our children the spirit of life.
This we know, the earth does not belong to us.
We belong to the earth.
This we know, all things are connected.
Like the blood which unites one family, all things are connected.
Our God is the same God, whose compassion is equal for all.
For we did not weave the web of life.
For we are merely a strand in it.
Whatever we do to the web we do to ourselves.
Let us give thanks for the web and the circle that connects us.
Thanks be to God, the God of all.

Chief Seattle, 1854.

The Genesis Story

A dramatic reading of Genesis 1:1-31

Reader #1: Before creation there wasn't much around, besides God, and nobody really knew what it was like. It might have been just nothing, a blank empty void, or it might have been full of...

Reader #2: Strings of purple, or...

Reader #3: Spots of green, or...

Reader #1: Dashes of orange...but, like I said, nobody really knows. It was around this time of timelessness that God decided to create the heavens and the earth.

Reader #4: Now the earth was formless and empty.

Reader #5: Darkness covered everything.

Reader #2: But the spirit of God was present.

Reader #3: So God said, "Let there be light," and the dark form of the earth was illuminated, and God could see what was going on.

Reader #4: And God was pleased.

Reader #5: Then God separated the light from the darkness. God called the light...

ALL: Day

Reader #2: And the darkness God called...

ALL: Night

Reader #1: And so then there was evening and there was morning,

ALL: The first day.

Reader #2: Then God decided there needed to be a little more form to what was already created, so God said...

Reader #3: "Let there be a huge space between the waters, separating them."

Reader #4: So God made this space, and there was water above and water below, and God called the water above...

ALL: Sky

Reader #1: And left the water below as just water for the time being.

Reader #2: And then, specifically because God created day and night, there was evening again and there was morning.

ALL: The second day.

Reader #3: Then God, looking at the sky, and at the water, noticed something more was needed. So God said, "Let the water under the sky be gathered in one place, and let dry ground appear,"

Reader #4: God called the dry ground...

ALL: Land

Reader #5: And called the gathered waters...

ALL: Seas

Reader #1: And at this point, things were looking pretty good and God continued to be pleased.

Reader #2: Seeing land and sky and seas, God figured this creating business was going pretty well, so then said, "Let things grow on the land: plants and seeds, trees with fruit and flowers of all kinds that will keep growing and reproducing."

Reader #3: And so all this vegetation sprouted, and the land became like a beautiful garden, and this God liked very much.

Reader #4: Then there was evening and there was morning

ALL: The third day.

Reader #5: During that evening time which was closing the third day, God thought there might be some confusion about what was actually day, and what was actually night, seeing as there was only light and dark, so God said, "Let there be lights in the sky to separate the day from the night; and these lights will be like signs to mark the seasons, days, and years."

Reader #2: So God made two great lights. The brightest, called the sun, would light the day and the dimmest, called the moon, would, sort of, light the night. God also made the stars.

Reader #1: And it was a very cool light show.

(continued on the next page)

Reader #3: And even more importantly there was a distinguishable evening and a distinguishable morning

ALL: The fourth day.

Reader #4: Then God decided that there should be more things on and around the earth than just plants and stars and lights, so God said, "Let the water be full of whales and fish and plankton and algae, and let the sky be full of birds and butter ies and mosquitoes."

Reader #5: And the excitement of all these living things was very good.

Reader #1: So God blessed them and told them to have lots of little whales and little birds and little butter ies to fill the water and sky.

ALL: So that the earth will never be without them.

Reader #2: And then there was evening, the first night that the birds and fish were tucked into bed, and there was morning, and the creatures were awakened with possibly the first rooster crow.

ALL: The fifth day.

Reader #3: And so in a great rush of pleasure at having created such beautiful and caring creatures, God decided to keep following the same line of thought and said, "Let there be living creatures to live on the land who will be...wild..."

Reader #3: "...and walk on the ground."

Reader #4: And so bears and cougars and mice and snakes and horses and elephants and all other animals and reptiles that you can think of started to walk all over the earth.

Reader #5: And it was like a big party, and God, with all the creatures, thought it was very good.

Reader #1: But God wasn't finished, and had been saving one very special creation until everything else was perfect and complete. Seeing that all things were ready, God decided the time was right, so God said, "Let there be people, woman and man, made in my image, and let them care for..."

Reader #2: "The fish in the sea,

Reader #3: The birds in the air,

Reader #4: The creatures of the land,

ALL: And all the earth."

Reader #5: And God blessed these two and said to them, "Have many children and grandchildren and great-grandchildren, so that you will never be alone."

Reader #2: And God taught the people:

Reader #3: "Live always in my love,

Reader #4: Share the beauty and wealth of my creation,

Reader #5: And care for each other and each living thing as I care for and love you."

Reader #1: And God looked over all that was created and probably giggled a little bit and did a little dance and thought that it was better than good, that it was better than very good, that it was, in fact, incredible.

Reader #2: There was evening, with a great deal of tucking in, and there was morning.

ALL: The sixth day.

Reader #3: And so, with the heavens and earth complete, and all things in their place

Reader #4: God, weary with delight and celebration, finally rested, and asked everyone else to rest too.

ALL: The seventh day.

Reader #1: And this day, God made holy.

Teach Us and Show Us God's Way

A Litany Prayer about the Earth

(Gather outdoors if possible. Practice the response: "Teach us and show us God's way.")

Leader: Let us pray. We call upon the earth, our planet home, with its beautiful depths and soaring heights, its vitality and abundance of life, and together we ask that it:

ALL: Teach us and show us God's way.

Leader: We call upon the mountains, the Rockies and the Olympics, the high green valleys and meadows filled with wild owers, the snows that never melt, the summits of intense silence, and we ask that they:

ALL: Teach us and show us God's way.

Leader: We call upon the waters that rim the earth, horizon to horizon, that ow in our rivers and streams, that fall upon our gardens and fields, and we ask that they:

ALL: Teach us and show us God's way.

Leader: We call upon the land which grows our food, the nurturing soil, the fertile fields, the abundant gardens and orchards, and we ask that they:

ALL: Teach us and show us God's way.

Leader: We call upon the forests, the great trees that reach strongly to the sky with earth in their roots and the heavens in their branches, the fir and the pine and the cedar, we ask them to:

ALL: Teach us and show us God's way.

Leader: We call upon the creatures of the fields and forests and the seas, our brothers and sisters the wolves and the deer, the eagle and the dove, the great whales and the dolphin, the beautiful Orca and salmon that share our Northwest home, and we ask them to:

ALL: Teach us and show us God's way.

Leader: We call upon all those who have lived on this earth, our ancestors, and our friends, who dreamed the best for future generations, and upon those on whose lives our lives are built, and with thanksgiving, we call upon them to:

ALL: Teach us and show us God's way.

Leader: And lastly we call upon all that we hold most sacred, the presence and power of the Great Spirit of love and truth which ows through all the universe...to be with us to:

ALL: Teach us and show us God's way. Amen.

Written by the youth group at Oak Bay United Church, Victoria, B.C. Canada.

The Right to Dream

Eduardo Galeano is a poet from Uruguay, South America. These are his "upside-down dreams" for a better world. The poem reﬂects many of his particular concerns about our world today.

Who knows how the world will be in 2025! But one thing is certain:
if we are still around, all of us will be people of the last century.
However, although we cannot divine the world that will be, we can well imagine the one we would like there to be. The right to dream does not figure in the 30 human rights which the United Nations proclaimed at the end of 1948. But if it were not for this...
the other rights would die of thirst.

Allow me, readers, the madness of inventing the future. The world which is upside down dreams that it lands on its feet:

In the streets, cars will be run over by dogs.
The air will be free of all the poisons of machines and there will be no
other contamination than that which issues from human fear and human passions.
The television set will stop being the most important member of the
family and will be treated like the ironing board or the washing machine.
The boys who don't want to do military service
will not be arrested – those who do, will.
People will work to live, not live to work.
No illness will be called mortal, because life itself is mortal.
Economists will not confuse the standard of living with the level of
consumption, nor the quality of life with the quantity of things.
Historians will not believe that countries enjoy being invaded.
Politicians will not believe that the poor enjoy eating garbage.
Cooks will not believe that lobsters delight in being boiled alive.
Street kids will not be treated like rubbish,
because there won't be street kids.
Rich kids will not be treated like money, because there won't be rich kids.
Education will not be the privilege of those who can pay for it.
Police repression will not be the curse of those who cannot buy it.
There will be no "legitimate" offspring and
"natural" offspring because we are all natural.
A black woman will be President of Brazil and another black woman
will be President of the United States of America. An Indian woman
will govern Guatemala; another will govern Peru. In Argentina, the crazy women of the Plaza de Mayo* will be exemplars of mental health, because they refused to forget in times of amnesia.

Reprinted with permission from *New Internationalist*, July 1995.

> * The "crazy women of the Plaza de Mayo" the author writes about are members of the Mothers of the Disappeared – women whose family members have been abducted by the police because of their involvement in the church, trade unions or humanitarian organizations and have simply "disappeared." The women frequently demonstrate in the plaza in front of the government and military headquarters, demanding to know where their disappeared relatives are.

Idea Page #5 Seasonal Celebrations

Group Check-in

What will day-to-day life be like when you're 70 or 80 years old? Hand out slips of paper and pens. Ask everyone to write down a prediction for when they're 75 years old – a prediction of something they would like to have happen that would affect their way of life then. Collect the predictions, mix them up, and read them out one by one. Which predictions seem unlikely to come true? Why? Which seem possible? Explain.

Easter or Pentecost T-Shirts

Here are some suggestions for painting and tie-dyeing T-shirts for the group:

- Put several layers of clean newsprint padding inside shirts to absorb excess paint. Have two people hold the T-shirt by the top and bottom (to keep material taut) while other group members place their palms in pie plates of fabric paint and "stamp" these on the shirt. Have everyone use fabric pens to sign their names!
- Create T-shirts covered in symbols of Easter or Pentecost (see page 152).
- Create special shirts to wear at the Pentecost worship service. Use orange, red, and yellow dye or paint to make   aming shirts!
- Try reverse tie-dye. Start with 100% cotton, colored material (jeans, socks, T-shirts – the darker the color the better). Secure rubber bands tightly around twists and bunches of fabric or fold accordion style and tie at intervals with string. Place tied garments in a chlorine bleach and water solution – a bucket of hot water and 2 cups (500mL) of bleach. Stir occasionally. Watch the color changes and remove when desired. The fabric will appear more faded when dry. Launder with soap before wearing. (**Note:** This is a strong bleach solution. Wear old clothes or you may end up reverse tie-dyeing more than you planned!)

Pentecost Wind Chimes

You will need: Baker's Clay (see recipe below), cookie cutters (optional), sturdy cardboard circle, nail, large blunt needle, scissors, string

Instructions: Using **Baker's Clay** (below) create chimes. Make shapes with cookie cutters or by forming them with your hands. Make fish shapes (a symbol of the early Christian Church) or shapes of symbols of the season (see page 152). With a nail, poke a hole through the tops. Bake them. Then tie one end of a length of string to the chime. Thread it onto a large needle. Push needle through the cardboard circle. Make a knot in the end of the string so it cannot be pulled back through the cardboard. When the chimes are all attached, create a loop of string for hanging the chime.

Baker's Clay

2 cups (500mL)   our
1 cup (250mL) salt
3/4 cups (190mL) water
2 Tbsp. (30mL) glycerin

Mix ingredients together.
Heat the oven to 300ºF (150ºC).
Bake objects (1/4in. or 6mm thick)
20-30 minutes.

Egg-cellent Games

Try these games at a group gathering, or host games for children of the congregation on Easter Sunday!

- **Egg Tapping.** The object is to see who has the strongest egg. The one with the last egg to break is the winner. Each player holds a hard-boiled egg in their hand so only the small end is showing. One player hits another player's egg hard enough to crack it but not so hard that their own cracks. Each time an egg breaks, the winner plays someone new.
- **Egg Pass.** Players stand in a circle, each holding a soup spoon. One player gets a hard-boiled egg placed on their spoon and must pass it to the person on their right. If the egg falls, the person on the right leaves the circle. Otherwise, the egg is passed on to the next person (on their right). The last person remaining is the winner.
- **Egg Rolling.** Clear the oor area. Roll one colored, hard-boiled egg toward the center. That egg becomes the target. Each player, in turn, rolls their egg toward the target. It's okay for eggs to bump other eggs. The winner is the player whose egg is closest to the target after everyone has had a turn.
- **Egg Racing.** Find a grassy slope for this game. Give each player a colored hard-boiled egg. Have them mark their eggs with a number or distinct marking for easy identification. Players roll their eggs down the hill at the same time. Award prizes for the egg that reaches the bottom first and the egg that rolls the furthest.

Alternative Egg Dyes

Try these ideas for natural egg dyes:
- Boil the papery outer skins of ordinary onions for 5 to 10 min. The more skins, the darker the dye will be. Strain mixture and throw away skins. Add 1 Tbsp. of vinegar to "fix" the color and make it permanent.
- Other vegetables such as spinach leaves and beets can be prepared in the same way as the onion dye.
- Strong tea, made with ordinary tea leaves or tea bags, makes a nice red-gold dye.
- The leftover water from boiling black beans makes a great purple dye.
- Experiment at will!

Eggs as Symbols

Eggs are an important symbol of new life both to Jews and Christians. One of the foods on the seder plate at Passover is the roasted egg – representing the burnt offerings made at the temple at major festivals. Eggs may also be a reminder of the salvation and new life the Jews began after they left Egypt. For Christians, the egg reminds us of the stone rolled away from Jesus' tomb, and so symbolizes the power of resurrection.

Hot-Cross Buns

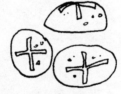

Make and serve hot-cross buns as a group project, as part of a special program for the whole church, or to take to shut-ins. This tradition began nearly 600 years ago when a monk in England baked special buns and gave them to the hungry. The story goes that one young man, too proud to accept the monk's charity, offered to take the buns and sell them in-stead. He sold all of them and when he came to worship, he put his earnings into the offering box.

Closing Worship

Related Scripture Readings: Matthew 28:1-10, Luke 24:1-7, John 20:1-10

Easter Ritual: In Greece, people use eggs as part of a special Easter greeting. When two people meet they hold out their eggs and tap them lightly together. One says, "Christ is risen" and the other answers "He is risen indeed." Perhaps it was from this tradition that the above **Egg Tapping** game originated. Give everyone a hard-boiled egg and explain how to exchange the greeting.

Prayer: Surprising God, you turn eggs into chicks, caterpillars into butterflies,
night into day, and sorrow into joy.
Help us understand the power of your love. Amen.

Retreats and Wind-Ups

Group Check-in

What is the most unforgettable experience you've ever had? Give everyone a chance to describe the feeling associated with this experience in a word or two – enjoyable, unpleasant, awesome, exciting, frightening. What made each one so unforgettable? Then ask everyone to name the most unforgettable experience that the group has had since it came together. Is there one experience that stands out for everyone or do different group members remember different experiences? What made the unforgettable group experience(s) so unforgettable?

Roll Call

Stand in a circle or line. Beginning with yourself, number off (i.e. "1, 2, 3,..."). Make sure people remember their number. Throughout the event, whether it's an evening or a weekend, do a head count and begin the roll call when you move to a new activity. Wherever they are, people respond by shouting their number in turn. If you're missing someone, you'll know!

Year-End Evaluation

Evaluate what you've done as a group over the year by brainstorming some possible questions (e.g. What have been high points and low points? What suggestions do you have for next year?). Choose a few to focus on and invite everyone to express opinions about them (either verbally or on paper).

How Do You Feel About...?

Rate the activities and dynamics of the group like Siskel and Ebert! Together create a list of the activities the group has done over the year. Include some general questions about leadership, ownership, and participation. Go through the list asking, "How do you feel about...?" before saying each one (e.g. How do you feel about...the worship services we took part in this year?). Encourage everyone to respond. This can be done non-verbally with just a "thumbs up" or "thumbs down." If you'd like more feedback, ask people to explain why they feel that way.

Tie-Dye Banner

Make a banner for a retreat or for the sanctuary for Pentecost. Use an old cotton sheet. Wrap rubber bands (or string) tightly around twists and bunches of the fabric. The fabric under the band will remain the original color. Follow the instructions on the package of clothing dye to mix (this usually requires hot water). Mix yellow and red dye separately in 5 gallon pails. (*Hint:* Adding a little salt will help maintain color fastness.) Place fabric in the dye until it is the desired color. (*Note:* Colors appear more faded when the material is dry.) You might want to begin with yellow and progress to red. The two will "bleed" to give you orange. Experiment with some test pieces before you begin dyeing the actual banner.

After each dip of the fabric in a color, rinse the material in cold water until the water runs clear. Remove the bands and re-tie it with string or rubber bands and repeat the process with a second color. Rinse thoroughly. When the material dries you can sketch images or the words on the material with pencil. Use fabric paints to color these in. Choose some sparkly fabric paint for an interesting, shimmering effect. If the lettering seems to get "lost" in the tie-dye pattern, outline it with a black permanent marker.

Comment Wall Mural

Tape sheets of newsprint to the wall. Write headings on them like "leadership," "worship," "games." Include any special categories that might apply to your group (e.g. retreat, Christmas Eve service). Put out the markers and ask everyone to write their comments under the corresponding heading. Afterwards give everyone a chance to read what others have written. (This can be a valuable tool for program planning for next year.)

Group Symbols

When people take trips to special places they often bring back keepsakes or souvenirs (e.g. pictures, a rock or shell, road map, pennant).

Using a variety of art supplies, invite everyone to make "souvenirs" of a special experience they've had in this group this year. The souvenir could be a symbol of something experienced as a group or as an individual in the group. When symbols are completed, gather together and invite everyone to present their souvenir, explaining what it symbolizes and placing it in the center of the circle.

Affirmation Bags

This works especially well as an early activity in a weekend retreat program.

You will need: 5 lb. brown paper lunch sacks, markers

Instructions: Give everyone a paper lunch bag. Ask them to write their name at the top. Then have them pass this to the person on their left. Give them instructions to draw a feature of that person (e.g. draw their nose). Continue to pass the bags on to the left, each time having group members draw another feature of the person whose bag they have. Depending on the size of your group you may have to include other features (e.g. something they are known to say, a distinguishing feature of their clothing). The bags are finished when they've returned to their owners. Remember, no one needs to be an artist to do this! The results? An outrageous composite drawing of individuals by other members of the group. Staple or tack these bags (opened) to a bulletin board and these become mailbags. Invite everyone to write notes of affirmation (e.g. thanking them for something they shared with the group, a compliment) to each other and place these in the bags. Encourage everyone to write to each member of the group at least once so no one feels left out. Distribute the mailbags at the end of the weekend.

Closing Worship

Related Scripture Passage: Mark 9:2-10

Reflection: Reflect on the transformations (personal or corporate) that have happened over your year together as a group. Name some of the things the group did together, some of the learning that individuals or the group experienced, some of the friendships that formed. Speak slowly with pauses to encourage others to name the things they remember and value.

Litany Prayer

Hand out copies of the following prayer and invite everyone to name things they are thankful for at the appropriate time in the prayer.

> **Leader:** For the friendships we have formed with each other over the year, Creator God...
> **ALL:** We give you thanks.
> **Leader:** For the time spent preparing ourselves for a life that is led by Christ, Creator God...
> **ALL:** We give you thanks.
> **Leader:** We are thankful for many other things...*(invite the youth to name people and things they are thankful for)*...We are thankful for so much more that you have given us but remains unspoken, Creator God...
> **ALL:** We give you thanks. Amen.

Idea Page #7　Group Closure

Group Check-in

Hand out sheets of paper and pens. Invite everyone to list a couple of events they are looking forward to this summer. Then ask them to make a paper airplane. Suggest they toss their paper airplane to someone else in the group, who then tosses it to someone else, and so on. Have everyone toss the airplanes on the word "Go." Then everyone picks up the one nearest them and tosses it to someone else. After a few minutes, have everyone pick up the plane nearest them and sit in a circle. Unfold the planes and take turns reading what people have written. Try to guess who wrote it.

Remember When...?

Sit in a circle. Imagine being with the disciples as they shared memories of Jesus. You might hear them say, "Do you remember when we went to the Temple with Jesus and he chased all those money-changers out?" or "Remember the boat trip we took with Jesus when that big storm came up, and we nearly drowned?" What other memories might stand out?

Though we never physically walked or talked with Jesus, we acknowledge that Jesus has been present with us as we gathered as a group this year. Invite group members to complete the phrase "Remember when...", recalling something you did as a group this year. The twist is: you must remember to include Jesus' name in the memory (e.g. Remember when we went on that ski trip with Jesus? Remember when we went swimming with Jesus and Terry did a belly-flop off the high tower?). Those who forget to use Jesus' name are out of the game. Continue until you're all out of memories.

Space Clean-Up

Clean up your group's special place – a room, a cupboard, a bulletin board. Remove any newsprint lists, artwork, and posters. Scrub the black marks off the walls, wash windows to leave the place clean and ready for use next year. Are there items that group members want to keep as "souvenirs" of the year?

Closing Affirmations

Hand out sheets of 11 x 17in. paper, fine-tipped felt markers, and safety pins. Invite youth to write, "Go out into the world and share your..." at the top. Leave lots of room for others to write on the page. Then help each other pin these sheets to the backs of their shirts.

Give everyone time to write something on each other's papers – an affirmation of a quality or talent that person has that they have shared with the group during the year (e.g. sense of humor, concern for others, insight). Then invite everyone to unpin their papers, read what others wrote, and reflect in silence on the following questions:

- Did any of these comments surprise you?
- Did anyone mention a quality or talent that you had never considered?
- How will you use these talents in the coming months?

Sharing Food and Memories

Share an **Agape Meal** (see page 146) like the early Christians did. Share a special treat and talk about your memories of the year together. Combine this with **Triggering Memories** on the next page.

Parting Wishes

Hand out slips of paper and pens. Ask everyone to write down a brief message to the whole group – a parting wish or advice. Collect these and mix them up. Then read the following, inserting their responses:

> After Jesus was resurrected, he appeared to his disciples – in the upper room, on the road to Emmaus, on the shore. But after 40 days he ascended into heaven. The disciples did not see him again. When he appeared to his disciples the last time, Jesus drew near and said to them, "...*(read one of the slips of paper)*... Go, then, to all peoples everywhere and make them my disciples...And I will be with you always, to the end of the age."
>
> (Matt. 28:19a, 20b)

Repeat until all the responses have been read. Don't worry if some of these are humorous – good-byes don't always have to be solemn occasions.

Triggering Memories

Gather in a circle. Place a number of items in the center that might trigger memories of group experiences over the year. Try to make them general enough that more than one memory can be attached to them. Some examples are a candle, a church bulletin, a measuring cup, a cotton ball, a marker. Encourage everyone to think both concretely and figuratively about these items. For instance, a candle might remind someone of the time you made candles as a group, while it might remind someone else of the warmth they've experienced from being with their friends. Have group members choose an item and hold it as they share their memory.

Sing a Song of Youth Group

Divide into small groups. Provide newsprint and markers, and ask each group to create a song that celebrates everyone's talents or recaps the year you've spent together. First, choose a tune that everyone on your team knows (e.g. "Twelve Days of Christmas," a favorite hymn, a popular song, a rap). Then brainstorm ideas. As group members come up with lines, write them on newsprint. Keep singing the tune to make sure the words fit. (See example in box below.) Invite the groups to take turns performing their songs.

> **The Twelve Months of Youth Group**
> (*Using the tune "The Twelve Days of Christmas"*)
>
> In the first month of youth group
> (*insert name of group member*) brought to us... e.g. one set of group standards and...
> On the second day of youth group...etc.
>
> (*Use as many verses as you need to include everyone in your group.*)

Adieu

Bid farewell to the places and things that have been part of your group this year or during your weekend retreat. Ask everyone to call out good-byes to things and people they'll miss. If this is the closing for a retreat, perhaps give everyone five minutes to rush from building, to beach, to fire pit, to washrooms yelling, "Good-bye..." When they gather again, ask them to list where they went.

Closing Worship

Related Scripture Passages: 1 Corinthians 16:13, 2 Cor. 13:13, 2 Thes. 3:16

Song and Prayer: Join hands by crossing your arms over each other and taking the hand of the person on either side of you. Sing your favorite song or say The Lord's Prayer. When finished, slowly raise your arms, turning out of the circle as you do, symbolizing your "going out" into the world. Then pass the peace. Go up to each other and say, "The peace of Christ be with you." Respond saying, "And also with you."

Simple song suggestion for Closing Worship page 113

(tune: Love, love, love your God)

Sis - ter, broth - er take your time go slow - ly.

Lis - ten deep in - side your - self, for ev - ery hour is ho - ly.

Game Card

Feature YOU-th Project

This is a great way for you to get to know youth on a personal, one-to-one basis and to help others in the congregation get to know them, too! Make sure both youth and parents understand what you are doing and why you are doing it. Phone to arrange interviews with youth in their homes if possible, or in another location if necessary. Make sure that parents know when you are coming. Advertise the project before it starts – in your church's newsletter, through announcements in church. Send a letter to all youth and their parents like this one:

Dear Youth and Parents,

I wanted to let you know about an upcoming project. (If, as you read this, you find yourself whistling the theme from "Mission Impossible" or "The Twilight Zone" this is completely understandable.)

My mission? To boldly go where no youth worker has ever been...to risk life and limb...to embark on a journey to places never before explored...well, you get the idea. I, YOUR FEARLESS LEADER, am coming to your bedrooms...er, well, sort of.

I will be encountering two members of the youth group each month. By encounter I mean I will interview you in your home (only if you are comfortable with that, of course!); I'll take some pictures of you doing some normal at-home sort of things; I'll meet your families, your pets, and ask some questions. Then I will feature **YOU** on the Youth Group Bulletin Board.

The goal? To get to know you better myself and to let other members of the congregation have a chance to discover some of the neat things there are to know about each of you. By meeting you in your own "space," I'll get to know you in a different way than I have through the youth groups.

I'll be letting you know more about this project soon.

Sincerely,

Your fearless youth leader

Some suggestions:

- Prepare a list of questions about favorite subjects, interests and hobbies, future plans, families, where they grew up – and anything else you want to know!
- Tape record your discussion with the youth. Then you don't have to be distracted from what they're saying by having to write things down.
- Encourage youth to show you their bedrooms, as this is where they likely spend a lot of time and these will say a lot about who they are, and their interests. Be sure it's O.K. with them!
- Encourage youth to show you photo albums, talk about trips they've taken, family holidays, and siblings. Make a point of meeting any family members who are around.
- Take photographs.
- Develop photographs and transcribe parts of the interview. Arrange text and photos on a half piece of poster board and display this somewhere where others in the church can read it.
- Afterwards allow youth or parents to keep these posters. (They may become treasured keepsakes.)
- Encourage the rest of the congregation to "check out" Feature YOU-th on the Youth Group Bulletin Board. Put announcements in the church bulletin or make verbal announcements in church to remind everyone about the project.

Youth Events Calendar

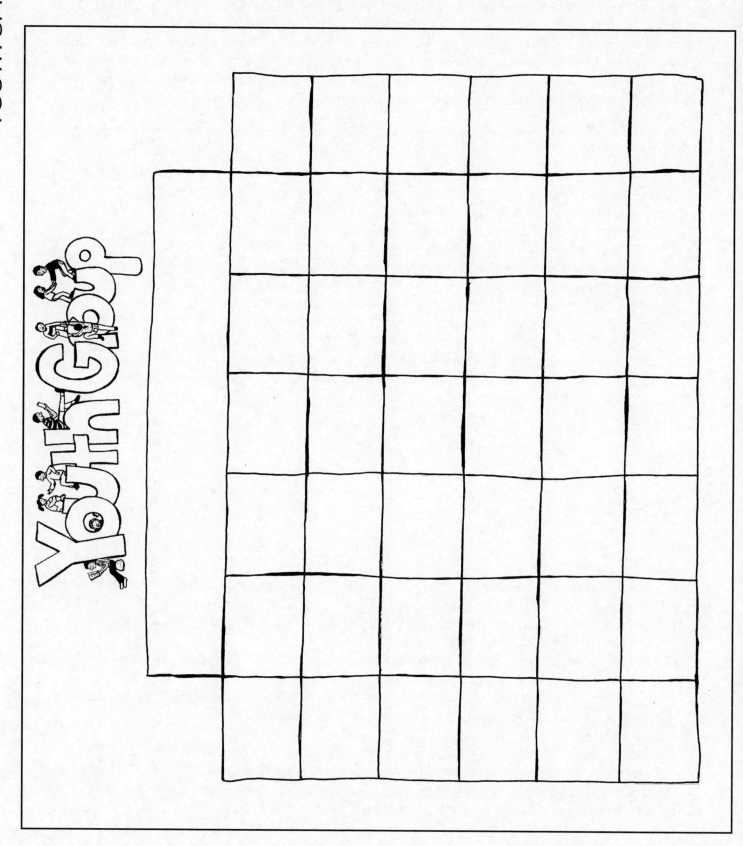

Service Project Ideas

Rake and Run

This is a service project youth really enjoy! On a given day, youth gather with rakes, pile into cars and go driving down the street looking for a lawn that needs raking. Members should go to the door and ask permission, explaining that there is no charge for this service. If permission is granted, all pile out and rake and bag the leaves. When the job is done youth might wish to leave a card saying "Best wishes from the youth group at _____." Another way to do this is to have church members identify lawns that need raking, those perhaps of seniors or shut-ins from your congregation. Then group members go to rake these particular lawns. After a couple hours of hard work, head back to the church for hot chocolate or refreshments. *Alternative:* In colder climes you might stage a "Shovel and Shove-Off" instead. This is a particularly strenuous activity for older folks who will certainly appreciate your efforts to make their walkways safe!

Scavenger Hunt

If your community has a food bank, shelter, or drop-in center for homeless people, contact them to see what items they need. Drop-in centers often provide clients with personal hygiene items and food that can be eaten without further preparation, as many clients do not have access to cooking facilities. Food banks will often have specific items they are lacking.

Create a scavenger list of 15 items or more. Contact members of the congregation (or place an ad in the bulletin the week before) describing the project. Ask for the names and addresses of those who might have some of these items or who are willing to pick them up during the week to have on hand when youth group members arrive to pick them up. Make a list of names and addresses. When the youth arrive, divide the group into several teams of three or more. Give each a list of items to collect and a list of names and addresses. This can be done as a "car rally" if you are covering a large area. Set a time limit and have groups meet back at the church to award prizes, have refreshments, and have a closing worship. If at all possible, have someone from the organization you are collecting for come and speak to the group briefly about the work of the organization and the people it serves. This can be a real eye-opening experience!

Note: You will likely want to limit groups to collecting only one item per household they visit. Explain to congregation members that there may be several groups visiting their home, they are only expected to donate one item per group, and that groups will be asking for specific items that are on their scavenger lists. You may also want to permit substitutions (e.g. if a group ends up with two tubes of toothpaste but no toothbrush) so groups don't turn down donations just because they've already collected that item.

Hamper Project

If your community is involved with a Christmas hamper project or has a food bank, arrange to have youth participate in the physical preparation of the food hampers —such as dividing bulk quantities into family size.

Easter Caroling

Caroling at Christmas is fun, so why not at Easter as well? Choose songs that communicate the Easter message. You can even get some flowers and give a flower to those to whom you sing. You may find that because it's unexpected, Easter caroling will go over even better than Christmas caroling. Arrange to sing at a nursing home, a hospital, or a residence for physically or mentally challenged people.

(continued on next page)

An "Alternatives" Project

Your group can support Bridgehead Trading or another Alternative Trading Organization by taking orders for Bridgehead products at Christmas, encouraging your church to use Bridgehead tea and coffee at its coffee hour, and by selling Rainforest Crunch (proceeds go to reforestation). It's possible to set up a wholesale account with which you can order items on consignment and pay for them or return them within 30 days. Consider ordering items to create a display of Bridgehead products at a Christmas bazaar and encourage people to "give gifts that give twice." Bridgehead will also send you a supply of catalogues for people to look through or take home with them.

For the Bridgehead outlet nearest you contact
Bridgehead
20 James Street
Ottawa, ON K2P 0T6
Call toll free: 1-800-565-8563

A similar organization in the U.S. is
Pueblo to People
1616 Montrose #3700

BRIDGEHEAD

Houston, TX 77006
Call toll free: 1-800-843-5257

Bridgehead Trading was formed in 1981, over a cup of coffee, by two ministers and two social activists. The idea really began with the coffee, and a realization that behind that coffee were poor workers, and an unfair system of trade. People worked for almost nothing, and poor countries remained caught in debt and injustice, while big companies made lots of money.

The four people began importing and selling coffee in their spare time. They paid a fair price directly to the producers. Bridgehead grew! It now sells $3.5 million worth of products every year. Coffee, tea, spices and Rainforest Crunch (a wonderful peanut brittle-like candy made with nuts grown in the Brazilian rain forest) and crafts from more than 23 countries are sold from mail-order outlets and stores across Canada. Fair prices are paid, and profits are given to the producer groups, used for interest free loans to new cooperatives and for reforestation.

Bridgehead is part of an international movement of Alternative Trading Organizations working to bridge the gap between wealthy and poor nations, through fair trade.

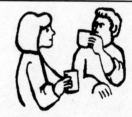

An announcement you might want to use to promote Bridgehead products in your church:
(Hold up a coffee bean between your first finger and thumb.)

Looks can be deceiving. Power doesn't always equate with size or physical strength. What I hold between my two fingers has the power to decide the fate of literally millions of people.

Now, if you have very good eyesight or if you're sitting in the front pew you may be able to see that what I'm holding between my fingers is a coffee bean. "How," you may be wondering, "does a coffee bean possess that much power?" The men and women of the developing world know the answer to that question only too well. They are the men and women who work on the coffee plantations funded and owned by companies such as Nestle, Hills Bros., General Foods, and Procter & Gamble.

We pay a lot for our coffee, but the real cost is borne by the people in the developing world. Not only are they exploited as a cheap labor force, in many cases they are also living in countries that export food while the majority of the population starves. Cash crops like coffee, sugar, cotton and the sale of beef generate national as well as private revenues while they gobble up the most fertile, productive lands and force rural peasants further into poverty.

Bridgehead is an Alternative Trading Organization run by OXFAM. It is dedicated to supporting its partners in the developing world by paying fair prices for the coffees and other products that it purchases.

With the Christmas Season approaching it's time to stock up on coffee and tea for holiday entertaining. What could be a better time to switch to drinking Bridgehead coffee?

Shrove Tuesday or Ash Wednesday Service

The Introduction

Reader #1: In the early Church it was customary to observe with great devotion the days leading up to Good Friday and the festival of Easter. It was a time in which new converts prepared for Baptism, in which those who had been separated from the Christian community by serious wrong doing were restored through repentance and reconciliation. It was a time when the whole community took part in a discipline of fasting and prayer and service.

Reader #2: Shrove Tuesday is the last day before Lent begins. On this day in former years, all rich foods – eggs, cream, butter, sugars – were removed from the house in preparation for the coming days of fasting. This food was often used up in making pancakes; thus it received the nickname "Pancake Tuesday."

Reader #3: "Shrove" comes from the Old English verb "to shrive" which means to make penance. Another name for Shrove Tuesday was "Fat Tuesday"; in French of course "Fat Tuesday" is "mardi gras."

Reader #4: Mardi Gras is still celebrated today; it usually consists of festivities – music, dancing, fireworks, and of course, indulging in very rich foods! The next day, Ash Wednesday, is the first day of Lent – a season that is marked by its thoughtful mood.

Reader #1: Lent is a time that prepares us for the celebration of Christ's Resurrection and renewal of our lives in Easter. We begin on Ash Wednesday by remembering our need for repentance, With the sign of ashes we begin our journey together to Easter.

Reader #2: Ashes are a symbol of the frailty and uncertainty of human life, and mark the penitence of the community. We are invited to begin this journey of faith through our confession of sin and commitment to again live out God's will in our lives.

Reader #3: The grace of our Savior Jesus Christ, the love of God and the strengthening of the Holy Spirit be with you all.

ALL (congregation): And also with you.

Reader #4: Let us pray. Most Holy God, we come to this Season of Lent with confession – saying we are sorry for disappointing you. We come to this Season of Lent with repentance – wanting to start over again to follow your ways. We come asking for new and honest hearts, and the healing power of your forgiveness. Grant this through Christ our Savior. Amen.

(continued on next page)

YOUTH SPIRIT

The Invitation

When the ancient Hebrews made public confession of their sin they would tear their clothing, put on sackcloth, and smear ashes on their head. This was a sign that they admitted their destructive patterns of behavior and were committed to new and life-giving patterns instead. In this service we are invited to be marked with the sign of our repentance and commitment to new life. We will be marked with ashes made from our own confession and from palm crosses that remind us of the ways we still act out a part in Christ's death. But we will be marked by the sign of the cross.

(Leader invites participants to take a slip of paper and pencil, and write down a characteristic of themselves that is hurtful to others or something they may need to let go of in order to improve their relationship with God or others. When they have finished writing, they fold these papers. Collect them and place them in a container along with dried palm branches or palm crosses from the year before if you have these. Burn the papers completely. Then add a little oil to the ashes.)

Preparation of the Ashes

In the early Church, oil was a symbol of healing. We mix these ashes, a sign of our repentance, with oil, a sign of God's healing love.

Prayer Over the Ashes

Leader: Loving and merciful God,
you have created us out of the dust of the earth.
Grant that these ashes may be to us a sign
of our mortality and need for your forgiveness.
Grant that the oil of your healing may remind us
of the gift you've given the world
in Jesus, your Son, who came to reconcile us to you. Amen.

(Pass the ash and oil mixture around the circle and invite participants to mark each other's foreheads with the sign of the cross saying "Repent and be renewed by the Good News of Jesus the Christ.")

Hymn: (tune of "Amazing Grace")

Forgive our sins as we forgive, you taught us, Lord, to pray;
But you alone can grant us grace to live the words we say.

How can your pardon reach and bless the unforgiving heart
That broods on wrongs, and will not let old bitterness depart?

Christ cleanse the depths within our souls and bid resentment cease;
Then reconciled to God and all, our lives will spread your peace.

Benediction

Leader: Go from this place in the strength of God's mercy to live and serve in newness of life.

ALL: We are sent in Christ's name!
Thanks be to God.

History of the Early Church

A Cooperative Game

Goal of the Game

The goal of the game is to get the group to move all the markers to the finish together by working cooperatively – just like the early Christians worked and lived together, sharing their wealth and possessions with one another for the good of the community.

Preparation

Although this game is designed to be played with four markers and an unlimited number of players, you may wish to make more than one copy of the game board and cards.

1. Prepare the game board by mounting the two halves of the board on poster board, fitting the two halves together carefully.
2. Cut apart all the cards and mount on recipe cards or lightweight cardboard cut to squares of 3 1/2 x 2 1/2 in. (9cm x 6cm).
3. Print "History" on the back of the History Cards and "Symbol" on the back of the Symbol Cards.
4. To complete the game board you will need dice and markers. Markers can be from another game, or use buttons or pennies.

Rules for Playing

1. Shuf e the deck of History Cards and place them face down on the game board where indicated. Place the pile of Symbol Cards face down where indicated.
2. Place markers on the START square. *(You can have 6 players but only four markers. If you choose to work with more players than markers, each player takes turns rolling the dice, selecting cards or moving. Remember, this is a cooperative game!)*
3. Player rolls one die and moves any of the markers ahead that many squares. If Player lands on a "History" square, select a History Card and read the information out loud. If Player is instructed to move forward or backward or go to Prison this should be done. The Player's turn is then over. If Player lands on a "Symbol" square, select a Symbol Card (half a fish). This card should be kept as it can be combined with another player's card to make a complete fish sign (see "Overcoming Obstacles" below).
4. Because **the object of the game is to have all players finish at the same time**, players can use their turns and Symbol Cards to help other players move toward the final square. **Players are not competing against one another.**

Overcoming Obstacles

- If a player is in Prison, another player must use their turn to roll a 2 or 5 to free the player. (A freed player begins again at the START square.) If a roll of something other than a 2 or 5 occurs, the player can still use that roll to move another marker on the game board.
- If a History Card tells the player they must have a complete fish sign before taking another turn, these cards should come from other players (who already have them in their possession or who land on the "Symbol" squares during play). As soon as two cards are matched together to form the symbol of the fish, the player is free to rejoin play. These Symbol Cards are then reshuf ed into the Symbol Card pile.
- While one player is waiting completion of the fish sign, it is possible, in the meantime, for other players to move any of the markers forward. However, until the player is freed to take their turn, there will be fewer players working together to move all the pieces forward.

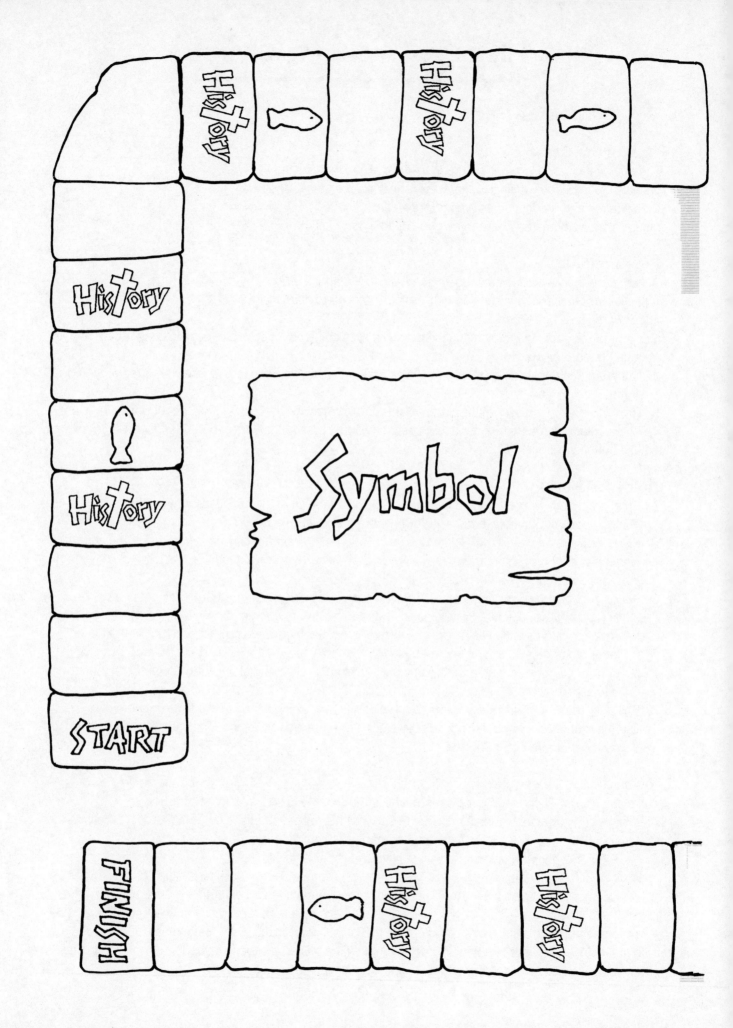

Symbol

Symbol

Symbol

Symbol

Symbol

Symbol

Symbol

Symbol

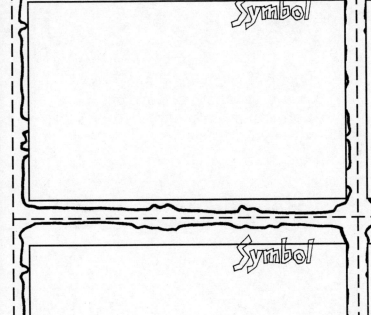

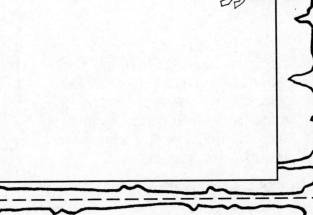

History

Attitudes towards women become increasingly oppressive at the end of the first century as the early Christians gradually gave up their hope for the early return of Christ and settled back into the traditions and customs of the world around them. It is within this context that the leadership of women such as Phoebe gradually diminished. **Go back 4 spaces.**

History

A number of young catechumens (those preparing for Baptism) were arrested (202 CE). Among them was Vibia Perpetua, a young woman of 22 years. She was married with a young baby. When she refused to make sacrifices to Roman gods or renounce her faith in Christ, Roman governor Hilarianus ordered her and her companions to be brought before the crowd in the arena and thrown to the lions. Perpetua and her companions survived the wild animals but were then killed by sword before the cheering crowds. Go to prison. **Another player must roll a 2 or 5 to free you.**

History

Phoebe, a deacon in the early church, was part of the Christian community in Cenchreae, near Corinth. She was a respected church leader who planned to travel to Rome. Paul wrote to the church in Rome to recommend her to them. **Move ahead 3 spaces.**

History

The early Christians live in community; they have "agape" meals—meals to promote fellowship and charity for widows, orphans and the poor. **Take a fish symbol card and roll again.**

History

You refuse to obey laws that demand your allegiance to Rome and worship of its emperor, and are forced to go into exile. **Lose your turn until you have a complete fish sign (two symbol cards).**

History

You are arrested and put in jail because of your beliefs. Go to prison. **Another player must roll a 2 or 5 to free you.**

History

John, in exile on the island of Patmos, has a series of visions which help to console Christians facing persecution. These are recorded in the Book of Revelation, the last book of the Christian Bible. **Move ahead 3 spaces.**

History

Peter preaches in Jerusalem (Acts 1:14–41) and three thousand are baptized and become members of the Church. **Move ahead 3 spaces.**

History

Lydia, a prosperous dealer in purple cloth in the city of Philippi, was the leader of the Christian community in her city. A "house church" gathered in her home. She helped fund Paul's journeys. **Move ahead 3 spaces.**

History

The Sadducees order Peter and John arrested for teaching people about Jesus rising from the dead. The Sadducees (a conservative sect of Jews) didn't believe in resurrection. Go to prison. **Another player must roll a 2 or 5 to free you.**

History

On the road to Damascus, Saul is converted to the Christian faith. Changing his name to Paul, he begins preaching in Damascus but soon begins traveling long distances to spread the good news with others. Paul founds many congregations like the ones he wrote to at Corinth and Thessalonica. **Move ahead 4 spaces.**

History

Paul is put in jail for his Christian beliefs. He continues to write letters from jail to the churches he has established in places like Corinth and Galatia, a Roman province in Asia Minor, encouraging them to remain faithful even in the face of persecution by the Roman authorities. **Move ahead 3 spaces.**

History

Paul is arrested in the Temple of Jerusalem and the crowd tries to kill him. **Go to prison. Another player must roll a 2 or 5 to free you.**

History

Prisca (Priscilla) and Aquila were a Jewish Christian couple who lived in Corinth. They were great supporters of Paul and traveled with him to Ephesus where they settled and founded a house church. Priscilla and Aquila also instructed Apollos, a Christian teacher from Alexandria, when he visited Ephesus. **Move ahead 4 spaces.**

History

The Roman Emperor Trajan (112 CE) declares that, if accused, Christians should be forced to give up their faith, worship Roman gods and declare their allegiance to the Emperor Caesar by saying "Caesar is Lord." Those who did not were punished. **Go to prison. Another player must roll a 2 or 5 to free you.**

History

By the beginning of the second century, many people were revolting against Roman law. Many different religions were attracting followers, and superstitious beliefs were spreading. Christians became scapegoats and were persecuted. **Go back 4 spaces.**

History

Ignatius of Antioch was seen as a strong pillar of the Church, which the Roman authorities hoped to undermine by getting rid of him. He was denounced, given a quick trial and taken off to Rome to be put to death. While on the way to Rome, Ignatius wrote seven important and moving letters which encouraged and inspired other Christians facing persecution. **Move ahead 4 spaces.**

History

The second generation of leaders in the church, though close in time to the apostles and their teachings, had to deal with different issues. The church was becoming more organized and began to ordain people to some positions of leadership. Bishop Clement, one such early leader, helped his people, who were being persecuted under the rule of Emperor Domitian, with words of encouragement and prayer. **Move ahead 3 spaces.**

History

The Roman people, many who were very superstitious, blamed social, economic and political calamities on the Christians—because they refused to pray to the Roman gods or to honor the emperor. **Lose your next turn.**

History

Envy and ambition are creating disharmony and threaten to cause divisions within the Christian community that you are part of. Several leaders in the community are competing for people's loyalty. **Lose your turn until you have a complete fish sign.**

Letters and visits by traveling Christians and missionaries help your community keep in touch with other communities of Christians. This is important because it is the only way you know what is happening to Christians elsewhere. **Take a fish symbol card and roll again.**

History

Christians helped one another by sharing all their wealth and possessions. Communities helped one another by sending money or other aid when possible. **Take a fish symbol card and roll again.**

When Christians traveled from place to place they were welcomed among groups of fellow Christians because they shared the same faith and might have news to tell about other Christian communities they had visited. This strengthened the sense of relationship between communities. **Take a fish symbol card and roll again.**

History

Polycarp, Bishop of Smyrna, was a church leader who had himself been a follower of the apostle John. Polycarp was arrested by Roman authorities. When he refused to abandon his Christian faith he was burned to death at the stake. **Lose your next turn.**

History

While gathered in Jerusalem to celebrate the Feast of Weeks (50 days after the Passover celebration) the power of the Holy Spirit was poured out on the followers of Jesus. The Christian Church is born. **Move ahead to the next History square and select another card.**

History

Through the apostles (and other traveling, teaching Christians), the Christian faith spread many places throughout the Mediterranean, into Africa and as far away as India. **Move ahead 4 spaces.**

History

Because of persecution against the Church, groups of believers were forced to worship in secret places, like the catacombs (underground tombs). **Lose your turn until you have a complete fish sign.**

History

Stephen, one of the first deacons in the church, performed miracles, preached the good news and made sure money and goods went to those in need. He was stoned to death by Jewish authorities who accused him of blasphemy. **Go back 3 spaces.**

Appendix

Annotated Bibliography

Books with Ideas and Resources for Youth Programs

Awesome Possibilities: User Friendly Programs for Youth Leaders. Program Resources Committee, Alberta Northwest Conference, The United Church of Canada, 1987 (3rd printing).
A packet of ready-to-use programs that includes helpful lists of goals, materials and preparation, and an agenda indicating length of time needed to complete each activity. The material is designed for medium size groups meeting for about two hours, but can be adapted to suit your particular situation. Most programs don't require much preparation time by leaders, and users have permission to copy many of the useful resources included in the appendices. Included in the package is *The Way of the Wolf* by Martin Bell, a book of modern-day parables that work well for closing worships.

Beyond Leaf Raking: Learning to Serve/ Serving to Learn. Peter L. Benson & Eugene C. Roehlkepartain. Nashville, TN: Abingdon Press, 1993.
This resource examines the "why's" of doing service projects with youth. It includes practical advice on how to choose a project, along with 135 project ideas ranging from international mission projects to local projects focusing on issues of poverty and homelessness.

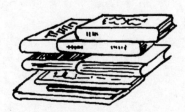

Building Teen Excitement: A Youth Worker's Guide. Shirley Pollock. Nashville, TN: Abingdon Press, 1988.
Here's 150 new and tried-and-true ideas for stimulating group communication, worshiping, doing outreach and fund raising. They build on many of the themes of the Christian Year. The ideas are especially good for those who like to "browse" through resources for ideas to build their own programs.

Energize! Energizers and Other Great Cooperative Activities for All Ages. Carol Apacki. Granville, OH: Quest Books, 1991.
Games for all ages and many ages together that encourage cooperation, participation, and fun! A helpful table of contents in the front of the book organizes games for "meeting and greeting," "growing as a group" and "racing and chasing," for groups with energy to burn! An alphabetical index at the back makes games easy to find by title. Use these to re-energize the group and bridge activities. These games foster a sense of belonging and cooperation – youth will love them and you can feel good about them too!

Get 'Em Talking: 104 Great Discussion Starters for Youth Groups. Mike Yaconelli & Scott Koenigsaecker, compilers. Grand Rapids, MI: Zondervan Publishing, 1989.
This resource not only provides ideas for creative ways to start discussions with youth groups, it also includes a helpful "Basic Training for Discussion Leaders." This is an introduction to using discussion as a tool to build community, stimulate and empower youth to action, and develop the relational skills of the youth in your group. The book includes a humorous "Discussions for Dummies" sort of trouble-shooter's index, in case

"they won't talk." An index at the front of the book lists group discussion starters by themes such as "Church" and "Parents."

Great Group Games For Youth Ministry: 94 New Fun-To-Play Games. Michael Warden, ed. Loveland, CO: Group Publishing, 1994.
This resource provides a range of games for small and large, indoor and outdoor settings in various kinds of weather – even a power outage! Pages include a useful margin guide to the number of players required and supplies needed to play these games. Games are grouped according to category (e.g. games for small places) in the front of the book.

Growing a Jr. High Ministry: Practical help for starting or revitalizing your ministry to young adolescents. David Shaheen. Loveland, CO: Group Books, 1986.
This resource offers a solid basis for building a ministry with young adolescents (12-15 years old). It includes information on the developmental stages of adolescence, and hints on finding volunteers, involving parents, and building your leadership skills. The final chapter includes 100 ideas for special events, retreats, and programs. These are "sketches" to develop and build on.

Idea-Log: Creative Ideas for Younger Youth. Donald B. Schroeder, compiler. Atlanta: General Assembly Mission Board, Presbyterian Church in the United States, 1979.
This resource includes 64 different activities designed for groups with junior-high-aged members. A process outlined in the Introduction (e.g. each activity lists objectives, planning process, creative options for implementation) makes this book user friendly. This resource includes a lot of ideas for projects that take a fair bit of preparation by leaders.

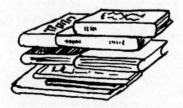

Live The Story: Short, Simple Plays for Churches. Cheryl Perry, compiler, Dianne Greenslade, ed. Wood Lake Books, 1997.
This resource includes 24 plays that can be used by youth in worship, as discussion starters or stand alone performances. The plays cover all celebrations from Christmas, Easter, and are organized according to the Seasons of the Church Year.

New Ways to Tell the Old, Old Story: Choosing & Using Bible Stories with Children & Youth. Delia Halverson. Nashville, TN: Abingdon Press, 1992.
Halverson explores the possibilities for creative storytelling through games, music and rhythm, cooking and eating, art, drama and writing activities. A helpful "Age Level Goals for Studying the Bible" for preschool children through adults is included in the Introduction. Many of the ideas are suitable for children and younger youth, though some may be adapted for a youth group setting. If you are leading a group of junior-aged, pre-adolescents this will provide many ideas for exploring Bible stories creatively.

Play It Again!: More Great Games for Groups. Wayne Rice & Mike Yaconelli, eds. Grand Rapids, MI: Zondervan Publishing, 1993.
This book pretty much covers it all – games for large and small groups, indoor and outdoor games, mixers, loud games and quiet games. There are lots of active, "physical, hard-hitting" games. The editors suggest that teams not be coed, but it may be better to base such a decision on the characteristics of your own group. Games are categorized (e.g. volleyball games) and an alphabetical index in the back makes games easy to find by title.

Psychology for Kids: 40 Fun Tests That Help You Learn About Yourself. Jonni Kincher. Minneapolis, MN: Free Spirit Publications, 1990.
A little far-out and a lot of fun! These exercises range from inkblot tests to either/or questions, and can provide interesting personal insights for people of all ages. These exercises may be more suitable for younger youth, but can be used as "stretchers" and "refreshers" for older youth, too.

Relational Youth Ministry: A Core-Team Model.
Mark C. McCann. Winona, MN:
Saint Mary's Press, 1995.
This resource includes surveys and exercises to help interested youth and adults shape, prioritize and plan a youth ministry program to meet their needs. This might be particularly useful for churches just beginning, or wanting to rethink, their youth ministry program and approach. Users have permission to reproduce many of the surveys and ranking exercises.

Books For Youth Leaders

Praying Our Stories: Reflections for Youth Ministers.
Daniel Ponsetto. Winona, MN: Saint Mary's Press, 1992.
For youth leaders who spend a lot of time theologically re ecting on the lives of young people, here's a resource with re ections on firsthand youth leader experiences! Ponsetto presents his own experiences in a humorous, re ective way, inviting readers to share their stories, too. Re ections on the work of youth ministry include "I Love These Kids: But Not Tonight!" and "Mr. Nice Guy or Sergeant Discipline: Which One When?"

Reviving Ophelia: Saving the Selves of Adolescent Girls.
Mary Pipher. New York: Ballantine Books, 1995.
Dr. Mary Pipher, a clinical psychologist, examines the effects of the media and a society obsessed with body image on the self-esteem and lives of young women. This is an eye-opening, revealing look at what it means to be young and female growing up in the '90s and how adults can help – a useful resource for youth leaders and parents of teenage girls.

Survival in Youth Ministry.
Robert J. McCarty. Winona, MN: Saint Mary's Press (Christian Brothers Publications), 1994.
McCarty approaches Youth Ministry as a new and developing ministry, one which is still "finding its place" in the church. The book deals with important questions of authority and power, practical strategies for "survival," and spirituality questions for re ection on your own situation.

Teen Trends: A Nation in Motion.
Reginald W. Bibby & Donald C. Posterski. Toronto, ON: Stoddart Publishing Co., 1992.
Drawing on their extensive national surveys, Bibby & Posterski discuss ten dominant directions young people are heading in today and the implications of these for parents, teachers, religious leaders, and youth workers. Although their research was conducted in Canada, many of their observations are universal in scope and will be useful for anyone in the Church working with youth.

Theological Themes of Youth Ministry.
William Myers. New York: Pilgrim Press, 1987.
As David Ng suggests in his Introduction, "This book is directed to the adult leader as a person...the youth ministry described here is not an ornate stage set literally constructed and begging for imitation." Myers presents and develops the theological themes of the Christian Year in a way that invites readers to imagine how these themes unfold in the lives of youth and how the church might meet them "where they're at." This is a quick read at 100 pages!

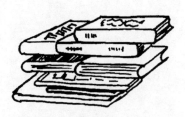

Season and Subject Index

Scripture Index